Administrative
Analysis

Administrative Analysis

An Introduction to Rules, Enforcement and Organizations

Christopher Hood
Professor of Government and Public Administration
University of Sydney

WHEATSHEAF BOOKS

First published in Great Britain in 1986 by
WHEATSHEAF BOOKS LIMITED
A DIVISION OF THE HARVESTER PRESS PUBLISHING GROUP
Publisher: John Spiers
Director of Publications: Edward Elgar
16 Ship Street, Brighton, Sussex

British Library Cataloguing in Publication Data
Hood, Christopher, *1947-*
   Administration analysis: an introduction
   to rules, enforcement and organizations.
   1. Public administration
   I. Title
   350   JF1351

   ISBN 0-7450-0187-4

Typeset in Times Roman, 11 on 12pt, by C. R. Barber & Partners
(Highlands) Ltd, Fort William, Scotland

Printed in Great Britain by Mackays of Chatham Ltd, Kent

THE HARVESTER PRESS PUBLISHING GROUP
The Harvester Group comprises Harvester Press Ltd (chiefly
publishing literature, fiction, philosophy, psychology, and science
and trade books); Harvester Press Microform Publications Ltd
(publishing in microform previously unpublished archives, scarce
printed sources, and indexes to these collections); Wheatsheaf Books
Ltd (chiefly publishing in economics, international politics,
sociology, women's studies and related social sciences); Certain
Records Ltd and John Spiers Music Ltd (music publishing).

Contents

Figures and Tables

Preface

Administrative analysis means the ability to think and argue systematically about alternative ways of providing public services. It is the next stop – the *pons asinorum*, perhaps – from straightforward narrative and description of institutional arrangements.

Even intelligent students sometimes have problems in crossing this bridge. Part of the difficulty, I think, is the lack of a general guide to administrative analysis which starts from first principles. There are many advanced-level monographs, histories of administrative thought, descriptions of the administrative arrangements of particular places, polemics, or treatments of some particular aspect of the subject, such as corporate organization. But where is the analytic 'ABC' of the subject to be found? This book is one man's attempt to fill that gap. As a teacher, I needed an introduction to the subject which was different from those currently on offer in that (a) it was analytically grounded rather than a chronology of thought in the field; and (b) it included a balanced discussion, rather than a curt dismissal, of the economics-based tradition of administrative analysis as against what until recently was the mainstream public administration tradition.

But I make no claim to originality. Anyone who writes a book like this is little more than a used idea dealer. Every part of this book is derived from other work, with a few minor glosses. What I am aiming for is to collect standard ideas and lines of argument together in a convenient form, which is reasonably accessible to the interested reader with no previous immersion in writing about public service provision. That does not mean that the subject can be reduced to the simplicity of a soap powder advertisement. Some parts of the chapters which follow may seem hard going to the novice, at least when read for the first time. I make no apology for that.

In order to do administrative analysis, you have to start with the basics and be able to go back to them in developing an argument. So the book starts by looking at the 'public service problem' literally from the ground up, using a very simple flood-control and water-supply example. After exploring the logical genesis of public service provision, the book moves on to consider three further elements of the administrative analyst's ABC, namely, the rule-making problem, the enforcement problem and the organization problem. The book then moves on to look at two sub-problems within organization: the adaptation problem in the provision of public services and the related problem of how far 'consumer sovereignty' can apply to public services.

The book has three main purposes. First, it aims to give the reader some sense of the 'administrative factor' in the organization of public services. Second, it aims to acquaint the reader with some standard lines of argument which relate to public service provision. Third, it aims to provide the reader with a simple tool-kit to enable him or her to think systemically about alternative ways in which public services can be provided. The reader is encouraged to develop this facility by a set of review questions at the end of each chapter, which require thinking about the ideas presented in that chapter.

I must acknowledge my debt to many students at the University of Glasgow and the National University of Singapore, who helped me to develop these ideas, by giving customer reactions from very different cultural backgrounds. Their negative or positive responses stimulated me to scrap or recast material which failed the consumer acceptability test, and to get out of blind alleys which I had been convinced were worth exploring. I am also grateful to several academic colleagues for their help. The idea of this book first took shape in my mind when I spent six months at the Institute for Interdisciplinary Research at the University of Bielefeld in 1982, where I was exposed to a number of fascinating perspectives on administrative analysis, in particular from Elinor and Vincent Ostrom, Giandomenico Majone, Reinhart Selten, Heinz Schleicher and Jim Sharpe. My intellectual debt to them will be obvious to those who know their way round this subject. As always, I am particularly grateful to my friend and colleague, Andrew Dunsire, for his patience and generosity in commenting on ideas in draft.

1 Administrative Analysis from the Ground Up: Public Goods, Public Power, Public Administration

'An ecological approach to public administration builds ... quite literally from the ground up.' (Gaus 1947, p. 8)

A fast-flowing river (R) runs through a low-lying coastal plain into a sea (S). S is:
 (i) stormy,
 (ii) shallow,
(iii) gravelly bottomed.
A sluggish stream (L), rising from a hill some distance away, flows into R near its mouth (M).

A small village (V) is set up on R's left bank between L and S. Two things make this settlement possible:

(a)   L is a source of potable water within reasonable carrying distance. R's water is salty near its mouth and so no good for that purpose.
(b)   A potential economic base. V is a suitable site for a logging station. Trees which have been cut from woods upstream can be floated down R to M, the logs collected and sawn at V, and the sawn timber shipped to other places. In time, other kinds of trade develop at V as well, particularly the building of wooden boats (as a means of turning raw material into finished goods).

What has this commonplace story to do with the provision of public services? So far, little enough. Let us say that V just happened, like thousands of similar settlements all over the world. It grew up within a general legal framework, notably of property and contract law. But no Economic Development Board planned it, no committee gave it a grant, no Ministry designated it as a favoured area. Indeed, let us go even further

1

S

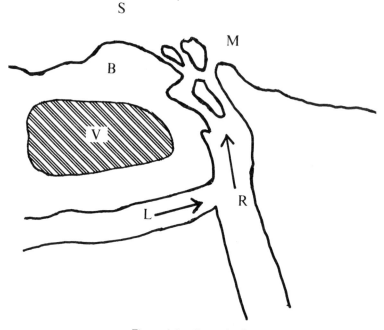

Figure 1.1   Coastal village

and suppose that V's inhabitants are all 'rugged individualists', who distrust government and public administration and wish to keep such forces out of their collective lives as far as possible.

THE RIVER-MOUTH PROBLEM

Even from this very scanty account of V, the reader will realize that making a living at V is living dangerously. Rivers and streams flowing through low-lying plains, as R and L do, will flood in times of heavy rain. A stormy sea like S will threaten a settlement on the adjoining coastal plain, for instance when a high tide combines with an onshore gale. Above all, the mouth of a river like R is bound to be unstable. A fast-flowing river will tend to carry debris (stones, sand, gravel) down to its mouth. This debris will tend to build up at the point where the river flows into the sea, forming a complex and ever-changing pattern of islands, bars, banks and watercourses. The gravelly bottom of S, continually shifting in storms, will interact with the river's debris. So there is an ever-present possibility that M will become partly or completely blocked for one reason or another (flash floods inland, gales and a high tide, or some mixture of the three). R will then seek a new outlet to S. This can normally be expected to happen at least once in a century.

It so happens that the first two dangers to V are less serious than the third. The risk of flood damage from L is limited by huddling V's houses close together on a low ridge above the top bank of L. Doing that, of course, itself creates other problems, as the reader will also recognize. Where buildings are crowded together, all are at risk if one of them catches fire through accident or negligence. Also, there are potential nuisance problems in relation to waste disposal that would be less acute in a widely-spaced settlement. It is difficult to cope with such problems without bringing in some degree of collective compulsion. But we shall ignore that for the moment.

The second danger to V, namely of coastal attack by S, is minimized by the presence of a natural bank (B) or sea-wall built up from the joint effects of the river's debris and the sea. Very occasionally, some sea water comes over B, in conditions such as were mentioned earlier. But the odds against a serious breach of B are fairly high.

The instability of M is quite another matter. V's inhabitants learned about the problem the hard way not long after V had been settled, when R found a new outlet to S to the left of M in a sudden flash flood, causing tremendous damage. The same thing could happen again at any time in similar circumstances.

Now flood control of at least a rough-and-ready kind is possible here. The risk of R seeking a new mouth can be reduced by widening M when debris begins to build up at M. With modern explosives, it is possible to blast M open to keep it where it is. Even if the worst happens, and M does become blocked, it is possible to blast M open again so that R returns to its original course. So the problem, though serious, is not insoluble. It is not one of those things that we just have to put up with. There is an available technology for doing something about it. But the application of that technology is neither automatic nor free. The skills and materials required are scarce and expensive. Somehow or other, the operation must be organized and paid for.

Limiting the flood threat to V posed by the instability of M is thus:

Feasible. The problem is at least in part soluble.

Important. The problem potentially threatens the lives of V's inhabitants, not just their comfort and convenience.

Collective. Inescapably, the solution benefits V's inhabitants *jointly.*

The last feature has considerable administrative significance. It is a bitter pill for our hypothetical community of individualists to swallow. It has three closely related implications.

(a) *Jointness of Consumption.* It is impracticable for V's inhabitants to get relief from the flood problem separately and severally – say, by setting their houses on stilts and buying a boat – however much they might wish to find that kind of solution. The unstable ground conditions caused by rapid water flow (remember that R is very fast-flowing) would soon undermine the foundations of such stilts if R did change its course to the left, quite apart from the probable difficulties of obtaining a reliable fresh water supply in such circumstances. Given that the only feasible solution to the problem is by blasting at M, it is not possible for any one person in V to protect his/her life and property by such operations without safeguarding everyone else's life and property in V as well. The benefit cannot be provided for one without being provided for all.

(b) *Non-Excludability.* It follows that if flood-control works are undertaken at M, it is not practicable to exclude those inhabitants of V who choose not to pay a share of the cost from enjoying the benefits of those works.

(c) *Indivisibility of Benefit.* It further follows that the benefit provided by flood-control works at M to one person in V does not diminish the benefits conveyed to others by these works, any more than one person's enjoyment of sunshine or moonlight inherently diminishes the amount of enjoyment available to others.

'Public goods' is the generic term normally used to describe cases where consumption involves these three properties. Discussion of the public good problem goes at least as far back as the famous eighteenth-century economist, Adam Smith (1978, pp. 25–6). The actual examples Smith used (the wayside fountain, the air) are perhaps slightly obsolete today, but public goods keep cropping up in new forms, as we shall see in Chapter 5. They do not fit into the normal assumption in law that property rights are exclusive and transferable or the normal assumption in economics that goods and services can be provided by voluntary market exchanges. Those assumptions can be applied to most of the goods with which V's inhabitants deal – the boats they build, the tools they use, the food they eat, the clothes they wear, the houses they live in. But there can be no exclusive or transferable rights to benefit from flood-control works at M, since the 'goods' cannot be denied to those who choose not to pay for them. Even if V's inhabitants prefer market dealings to collectivist action as a general rule, they must make an exception when it comes to physically protecting their property against flood. The most that can be done by individual action is to provide emergency apparatus, such as boats or amphibious vehicles, or individual insurance cover, as means of coping with a leftward shift of M. Even 'individual' insurance cover, of course, requires a community of insurers amongst whom risks can be pooled, and that can be problematic if most people decide not to insure. In any case, such expedients deal with the consequences of floods, not with the causes of the problem.

In the absence of a market solution to the provision of flood prevention works at M, there are three ways in which such works might be undertaken and paid for.

(1) *Voluntary Collective Provision.* V's inhabitants might band together voluntarily to pay for the works, from a common feeling of shared danger. With a very small community faced with such a threat, this is possible. V, as a settlement of a few hundred persons, might perhaps produce this kind of uncoerced solidarity. But what if, after all, there are people who refuse to pay their share? As we have seen, the service if provided cannot feasibly be denied to those who choose not to

pay. Some people may conclude that the smart thing to do is to enjoy the benefits but to let others bear the cost of the common works. This is usually termed the free rider problem (see Olson, 1971, pp. 9–16). Propensities to free ride can be catching – Why should I pay if you won't pay? One person who chooses to hold out can start a chain-reaction, and the whole effort to provide the works by joint voluntary action is highly vulnerable to collapse under free-riding pressure.

(2) *Voluntary Provision* by one or a few people. If one or a few people stand to benefit enough from stabilizing M, it may be worthwhile for them to pay for the whole cost of the works, even if everyone else in V chooses to free ride. For instance, if 75 per cent of the houses in V belong to a single landlord, that landlord may well decide to carry out the flood control works on his own in order to protect his own investment, even if there is no way that he can make the owners of the other 25 per cent of the houses pay towards the benefits that he is providing them for nothing. But the more evenly distributed is the ownership of real estate in V, the less likely it is that things will be done this way. If costs are high, the benefits of public good provision have to be concentrated in order for there to be an incentive for one or a few of the potential beneficiaries to provide them alone.

(3) *Coercion.* If neither (1) nor (2) will serve, the only other possibility is to base the flood-control work on some kind of coercion. Provision is financed by taxation – using that term to stand for any kind of payment which is compulsory. Punishment is visited on individuals who do not pay the tax.

The adoption of method (3) brings 'public administration' into this arcadian scene. V's affairs cease to be regulated by general laws of contract and private property alone. That administration is 'public' in two senses. First, it deals with the provision of services which have some or all of the properties of public goods as defined earlier. Second, it involves the use of the 'public power' – the generic Roman law term for the legal power to command, forbid, permit and punish (*imperare, vetare, permettere, punire*).

THE WATER-SUPPLY PROBLEM

The prospect of collective ruin by flooding is not the only water-related problem that affects V. Look at its fresh water supply. We saw earlier that one of the things which made V possible was the fresh-water stream (L). It was also noted that L is sluggish. The reader will have seen the significance of that. The capacity of a stream to break down pollution (known as biological oxygen demand) depends on how fast it flows. That means that L is highly vulnerable to pollution. So if those living upstream on L use L for a drain while those living downstream use it to gather water, the result is dismally predictable. There will be an epidemic of water-borne diseases, such as cholera or typhoid.

This is an instance of what is more generally termed the 'tragedy of the commons' – that is, the degradation of a common resource by incompatible use (Hardin, 1968). We might possibly imagine that in this case a common recognition of the problem might lead all users of L to stop polluting it for reasons of public-spiritedness. In a small community, where everyone's doings are closely observed by everyone else, this might happen. On the other hand, it is quite possible that each individual user might reason like this:

(a)   Even if I hold back from polluting L (say, by burning or burying refuse, or by installing septic tanks), others are unlikely to do so. So all my considerably personal cost and inconvenience will in the end probably be wasted, since L will still be polluted.
(b)   Alternatively, if everyone else *does* stop polluting L, the small amount of pollution that I individually create in L is unlikely to cause a catastrophe.

Of course, if everyone reasons and acts in this opportunistic fashion, the common resource will be degraded even if the underlying problem is well understood by each user, and each user would much prefer the resource not to be degraded.

This problem is far from trivial, but it is not exactly the same as the flood problem. It is just possible to imagine people providing for themselves as individuals other than by insurance alone – for instance, by buying pure bottled water or water from carts, by sterilizing water taken from L and/or walling themselves up in hermetically sealed houses so as to escape infection. Individualized 'private good' solutions to the problem are in this case inconvenient (tedious, laborious, expensive), not fundamentally impossible.

Beyond that – following our assumption that V is populated by people who prefer 'individualist' solutions of their problems – we might contemplate legal remedies or contracting solutions. The precise legal remedies available will depend on how the law in this case assigns liability in cases of incompatible uses of a common-pool resource (the basic problem here). 'Downstreamers', for example, might raise actions against 'upstreamers' for unreasonable use of L, if the law of nuisances follows a 'reasonable use' application. The snag with that approach lies in the (probably) intractable difficulties of accurately identifying the polluters.

A contracting approach would probably be equally clumsy, if not more so. It might in principle be possible for those living downstream to purchase covenants from those upstream not to foul L's water – to buy out their pollution rights. But there are at least three difficulties in this solution. First, the cost of conducting such transactions would be immense, even in a community as small as V. Suppose there are a hundred proprietors involved, spaced at intervals down L's top bank, and that each must enter into an individual contract with every proprietor upstream of his property. That means that 4949 separate contracts would have to be negotiated.

Second, an even more serious problem is that strategically placed proprietors might be in no hurry to come to terms, in the absence of moral pressure (such as might apply in the middle of a raging epidemic). Obviously, the longer they held out while others settled, the more valuable their covenants would become in order to complete the set (on the assumption that the set of covenants would be worthless unless 100 per cent complete). Indeed, the proprietor furthest upstream would be in an almost impregnable negotiating position to hold out for the most exorbitant sum from the other 99. We might expect endlessly protracted negotiations and extortionate demands by those who held out the longest. There is a distinct possibility of deadlock in such a situation. Third, even if such difficulties were overcome, the bargains were struck and the covenants signed, how could the contracts be enforced? We are back to the difficulty of identifying sources of pollution which arises under the nuisance liability approach considered above.

Short of everyone – or at least the 99 'downstream' households – living on bottled water, there is a technologically feasible alternative. Fresh water from elsewhere (for instance, from further upstream on R where R's water is not salt) might be piped to V. Such an undertaking would require the installation and maintenance of at least one water tower and pumping gear (the land, remember, is low-lying) as well as the laying of a run of pipe and the negotiation of rights to take water from R. Of course, such things do not come free. Once again, issues of payment and organization arise.

A piped water supply is not a public good in the same sense as the flood-control works at M. Assuming that supply is to individual houses rather than to a common standpipe, payment can be demanded as a condition for households being connected to the supply pipe. Those who do not pay can be cut off. If water meters are installed, payment can be directly related to use. Some degree of jointness of consumption is thus involved, but not non-excludability nor indivisibility of benefit. If the supply of water from R is finite, the more that one consumer uses, the less is available to others.

Nevertheless, two difficulties can be expected if the venture is undertaken within the general framework of contract and property law alone. First, in order to lay its pipe, the water-supply enterprise must negotiate easements or servitudes with everyone whose land the pipe must cross to get from R to V. There is here a potential for exactly the same difficulty as arises with the contracting solution to the pollution of L. That is, opportunistic proprietors have every incentive to drag out negotiations and avoid coming to terms. The last proprietor to settle in order that the run of pipe can be completed will be able to hold the water-supply undertaking to ransom, demanding a sum far above what would otherwise be the market value of that right. This is the holdout problem again.

Second, there are not likely to be rival piped water suppliers competing for the custom of V's inhabitants in the same way as there might be competition to supply them with bread or boots.

The first enterprise to lay a network of pipes would be in an almost impregnable position against rivals. Even if householders were willing to have two or more separate water pipes coming in to their houses (and they might well be, if the original water company's tariff became high enough), the heavy capital cost of installing duplicate plant and of negotiating servitudes would be difficult for rival suppliers to recoup. The original water company would be able to buy rivals out if they posed a credible threat. It would be well placed to strangle them at birth by cutting its tariffs temporarily below cost, removing the incentive for its customers to switch suppliers and removing the possibility for its rival to recover the cost of setting up an alternative supply. This tactic of 'predatory pricing' is based on the expectation that the original monopolist can recoup temporary losses by returning to its 'normal' exploitative tariffs after it has seen off the opposition. Even when piped water supply begins (as it did in London) with multiple pipes laid by rival companies running down the same streets, the logic of the situation tends to lead quickly to monopoly (cf. Crain and Ekelund, 1976, p. 153).

This is another case of solving one problem and creating another. Having dealt with the water pollution problem, V's inhabitants run the risk of coming under the yoke of a rapacious monopolist, normally charging as much as it can for its services and imposing what amounts to a heavy tax on V's inhabitants for something they can scarcely do without.

Once again, starting literally from the ground up, we come to fundamental problems (that is, problems basic to the sustenance of human life) that cannot be satisfactorily tackled without some form of public administration which goes beyond the general law of contract and property. That applies even if that general law is taken as the normal framework within which services are provided and stringent arguments are required for departing from that framework. At the minimum, the provision of piped water from R to V requires the overriding of individual property rights by some device for breaking the power of 'holdouts'. Some device is also likely to be needed to stop the water supply enterprise from exercising to the full its power to exploit its captive customers in tariffs and in matters such as terms for supply and repairs. Once again, the 'public power' can hardly be prevented from entering the picture, even though we are no longer dealing with a pure public good in the strict sense of the term.

OTHER SOURCES OF INTERDEPENDENCE

An account has been given of the forces which lead to the use of the 'public power' to deal with collective problems, even in a community like V, which is assumed to have strongly anti-collectivist leanings. These forces basically spring from (1) human interdependence in the use of resources, coupled with (2) a sizeable degree of self-regarding opportunism among the people affected. In such conditions, voluntary exchanges and contracts work clumsily or not at all as a means of providing some crucial services.

We saw three kinds of interdependence-derived problems in V's story. The flood control operation combines joint consumption, indivisible benefits and infeasibility (or very high cost) of exclusion. This is the extremest kind of interdependence. The piped water-supply operation involves less interdependence: joint consumption, but benefit is divisible and exclusion is feasible. Some use the term 'toll good' to label this kind of hybrid (see Ostrom and Ostrom, 1978, pp. 12). The pollution of L is a tragedy of the commons problem stemming from incompatible use of a common resource. The difficulty involved in negotiating agreements not to pollute L or to lay a water pipe from R to V is what is known as a transactions-cost problem. Theoretically, we could imagine the problem being solved by voluntary agreement. But the probability of deadlock is high because in this case the transaction requires the agreement of a large number of parties, any one of whom can hold matters up indefinitely by dragging his feet. (Transactions costs more generally mean the costs of arriving at any kind of exchange, in terms of the time taken in negotiation, the costs of acquiring relevant information, costs of enforcing contracts etc.)

These are not the only possible kinds of human interdependence in resource use (see Schmid, in Samuels and Schmid, 1981, pp. 76–94). For instance, scale of provision or the total quantity of demand may affect the average costs of supply. Take the average cost of maintaining a given level of water pressure for all customers connected to V's supply pipe. This cost will be far higher if demand is bunched than if it is spread out – for instance if (to take an exaggerated case) every household chooses simultaneously to take a bath, run the washing machine, hose down the car and water the garden at exactly the same instant. This is a peak-demand problem familiar in services such as power generation, telecommunications, transport facilities.

Even without that kind of problem, the number of customers may affect the average cost of provision. For instance, suppose that for some reason V's population suddenly trebles from (say) 200 to 600. The cost per person of the flood-control works ought to fall proportionately, since the total cost of controlling M is not related to population size. But water supply is a different matter. At some point, extra population will mean hiring more hands, building more or bigger water towers, installing extra pumping facilities and larger gauge pipes, such that average cost of supply may well rise at some points. Many urban public services today involve increasing costs to scale (see Schmid, in Samuels and Schmid, 1981, p. 84). In principle, such scale-of-operation interdependencies can be handled by voluntary exchange or market-like processes, such as peak-time pricing rules or differential tariffs (higher water charges to new settlers, for instance) – but as a matter of fact, they often occasion political pressure for cost averaging or tax-based provision.

THE PUBLIC ADMINISTRATION PROBLEM

The mundane problems of V have been used as a simple example of the way in which public service provision can be looked at from the ground up. Even in a small, simple settlement such as V, we come quickly to problems of a rather fundamental type which (a) are faced by a community jointly; and (b) given opportunism, can only be tackled by using the public power to supplant freedom of contract or voluntary provision.

In larger, wealthier or more complex settlements, such problems tend to multiply. First, bigger scale tends to throw up more incompatible-use problems. The incompatible use of air for breathing and for burning fossil fuels is not likely to be much of an issue in a small coastal village like V, with say 100 smoking chimneys. But if V grows to the size of London or New York, with millions of such chimneys, the incompatibility becomes dramatic and visible. The same goes for matters such as traffic congestion and parking behaviour. Second, increasing wealth creates possibilities of new kinds of public or joint-consumption services that are beyond the resources of a subsistence-level economy. Examples might be attempts to beautify V's public places or to delight the collective senses of its inhabitants – such as tree-lined boulevards, coloured street lights, publicly displayed works of art, processions, carnivals and pageants in the streets. These are 'luxuries', not life-or-death matters like flood prevention, but they are public goods too and their provision presents exactly the same collective-action problems. Third, social solidarity tends to decline as communities grow larger, richer and more heterogeneous. The voluntary collective action approach to public goods and related interdependencies is less likely to succeed and the use of the public power to deal with opportunism becomes unavoidable.

The public administration problem is thus one of devising and enforcing rules to govern the consumption and production of such services. In the organization of consumption, the problems to be solved include the use of the public power 'to foreclose the holdout problem and to provide arrangements for levying taxes or coercing user charges from all beneficiaries comprising the joint-consumption unit' (Ostrom, 1975, p. 691), to regulate incompatible-use problems and to allocate rights in scale-cost interdependencies.

Of couse, as Ostrom (1975) also points out, the substitution of authority for uncoerced agreement, taxation for voluntary payment or exchange, potentially means a loss of information about demand. It may give an opportunity for citizens to exploit one another. It may enable those who wield the public power to throw heavy costs onto consumers, regulatees, taxpayers, to enrich their friends and punish their enemies. In market exchanges, demand is signalled by the prices that customers will pay for a given quantity or quality of goods. But that cannot be used to fix the quality and quantity of public or other goods to be supplied under a tax regime. For instance, in deciding between a cheaper flood-control operation with a higher risk factor and a more expensive one with a lower risk factor, voting or some other means of expressing preferences must be used. Real consumer choice problems start to arise.

Moreover, as we go from the unambiguous life-and-death problems (potable water, flood protection) to the collective consumption of 'luxury' items, the more difficult are likely to be the decisions on quality and quantity of supply, and indeed the more likely it is that one man's public good cost-sharing problem is another man's incompatible-use regulation problem. For instance, suppose that V grows so prosperous that art works might be put on every street corner and top-rank performing artistes hired to play in the streets for the amusement of passers-by. To those whose tastes are served by such activities, they are public goods in exactly the same way as flood-control is. To those with opposite tastes (say, those who dislike art works or prefer peace and quiet as they go about their business), they pose an incompatible-use problem in exactly the same way as pollution of the stream L. Somehow, rules must be devised to handle demand decisions as part of the process of organizing consumption.

Second, production of the goods or services involved must be organized in some way. What alternative modes of organizing the work are available? What tasks must be performed and in what order, surmounting what difficulties, before we move from the *idea* (of controlling M or piping water from R to V) to the actuality?

The rest of this book builds on the issues which have been sketched out here.

1. If the outcome of public service problems like those discussed earlier depend on the rules which govern the situation (for instance, in opening up or foreclosing the possibility of holdout behaviour), the public administration problem can be seen as a rule-design problem. The next chapter looks at rules in general and at some of the issues which arise in 'designing' rules.

2.   Rules can be expected to shape behaviour only to the extent that they are enforced. Once we come to the *public* power and depart from *voluntary* collective action, *enforcement* of the rules becomes a central theme in administrative analysis. Chapter 3 explores rule enforcement.

3.   Chapter 4 moves from rule design and enforcement in general terms to consider some more specific choices in organizing public services.

4.   Chapter 5 looks at the way in which public services can be adapted to changes in supply and demand. The problems to be dealt with, and the available means of dealing with them, can easily alter with shifts in social behaviour or population density, new technology, or changes in the natural world. At the same time, information about demand can easily be blanked out (as noted above) where the public power is used to organize public service provision. Adaptation in public services therefore merits some separate attention.

5.   Chapter 6 picks up issues that have already been raised (and recur in the chapters which follow), by looking at the extent to which a 'consumer sovereignty' principle can or should apply to public service provision. Where consumer sovereignty is impossible, can public services be made 'user-friendly' and, if so, how?

QUESTIONS FOR REVIEW

1.   It was noted that huddling V's houses close together (to minimize risk of flood damage from L) created a collective fire hazard and a potential nuisance problem. Would fire-prevention measures (such as prohibition of thatched roofs) and nuisance-control measures (such as night-soil collection) be public goods in the same way as controlling M by blasting operations?

2.   Would you expect the incidence of public services based on public goods or other kinds of resource inter-dependencies to increase in V (or any other community) as V became larger, richer, more sophisticated?

3.   Can technological change produce *new* public goods or

transform what were once public goods into goods capable of being bought and sold through ordinary market processes? Can you think of examples?

4.   In what sorts of cases, if any, might you expect public goods to be provided *other* than by the use of the 'public power' of compulsion?

5.   Should the public power be used for the provision of goods other than public goods – for instance, in compelling travellers to take out insurance against costs of medical treatment abroad or loss of baggage before they are allowed to leave their own country?

GUIDE TO FURTHER READING

Gaus (1947, pp. 8–19) discusses how administrative analysis can be taken from the ground up. The style is now a little old-fashioned, but it conveys well the spirit of that approach. For issues connected with public goods, holdouts and free riders, a good introductory book is Laver (1983, esp. pp. 17–46). Fuller discussion of the subject and classifications of types of goods and situations can be found in Olson (1971, esp. pp. 9–16, 53–65), Posner (1977, esp. pp. 125–91), Ostrom and Ostrom (1978, pp. 7–49), and Schmid (1981, pp. 76–94). All these sources have been heavily drawn upon here.

2   Laying Down the Law: Making Rules and Regulations

'If it's small you pick it up. If it's large you paint it white. If it moves you salute it.' (old military saw)

I. WHY RULES?

Suppose that it is decided to set up a multi-person local flood commission for V. The commission's general task is to control M, and it is to exercise some degree of public power for that purpose – in raising taxes, for instance. Here are six of the issues that might have to be resolved as that general idea came to be translated into specifics. They come from a useful categorization of types of formal rules by Ostrom (1984, p. 26), who has identified six types of rules as the 'DNA' or basic genetic structure of any decision situation *whatever*.

First, who exactly is to be involved in these arrangments? Who is to be liable for tax? Where are the boundaries of the tax district to lie? Who is to be eligible for the office of flood control commissioner? (Should the office be held by local people only, who know the local situation? Or is it more important to have people with qualifications in, say, hydraulic engineering, irrespective of where they come from?) These matters relate to what Ostrom calls *boundary rules*.

Second, what should the powers of the commission be? What taxes might it levy, how often and within what limits? What works might it carry out? Should its powers and duties relate to the management of M only, or include sea-defences against S and flood-limitation works for L? Such questions refer to what Ostrom terms *scope rules*.

Third, how many commissioners should there be? Who

should appoint, elect or dismiss them? How long should they serve? Should all have equal responsibilities, or should some of them have special powers and duties (e.g. chairman, secretary)? *Position rules*, in Ostrom's language, are at issue here.

Fourth, how should tax assessments be made, in matters such as notification, valuation formulae, scope for appeal? What should be the procedure for binding the commissioners to transactions? How should contracts be entered into, for instance in competitive tenders and public advertisement? Should the commissioners be able to delegate their powers and, if so, when and how? Such matters are the province of what Ostrom terms *authority and procedural rules*.

Fifth, what records and accounts should the commissioners have to keep? Should there be any confidentiality about their work? What reports should they issue, to whom, and at what intervals? Should they be required to declare any interests in matters to be dealt with by the commission? Should tax assessments be open to public inspection? What information or returns should taxpayers be obliged to provide for the commission? Such questions relate to what Ostrom calls *information rules*.

Sixth, how should the commission arrive collectively at a decision? What would be a quorum? If there are disagreements among the commissioners, should they be resolved through majority voting of some kind, or in some other way – for instance, by placing ultimate authority in a chief commissioner, by someone's 'sense of the meeting', or even by unanimity? If there is to be a chairman with a casting vote, how should that vote be exercised in the event of deadlock (for instance, in favour of the status quo)? If the commissioners are to be elected, how should that be done? These questions relate to what Ostrom calls *aggregation rules*.

These are, of course, lawyer-like questions. They concern the formal rules within which the public power is exercised or public services are provided. If V were populated entirely by lawyers, we might imagine a structure of highly elaborate rules being devised from the start to cover all of these matters, and perhaps many others as well. But even if V consisted entirely of relatively easy-going people, generally averse to 'lawing', *some* formal rule-making of this kind can hardly be avoided. It only takes some element of opportunism and/or honest disagreement (the source of the service provision problems identified in the last chapter) to enter the scene, to set off demands that the rules be spelled out.

The more opportunism and the more disagreement there is, the more elaborately articulated the rules will have to be. But even if there is absolutely no opportunism or disagreement in the case, reducing matters to rule can have advantages in saving time that would otherwise be taken up in discussion. Instead of long deliberations on what is wanted every time something needs to be done, time and resources can be saved by adopting rules which are followed automatically in particular circumstances, unless it is agreed to set the rules aside.

These are the reasons why rule-making is basic to administrative analysis and why the design and enforcement of formal rules is central to what administration is ordinarily taken to mean – ordinarily, in the sense both of popular understanding (cartoons, comedy routines) and of conventional academic accounts. So this chapter looks at some ,issues involved in rule-making. The next chapter looks mainly at rule enforcement. These are, of course, merely two aspects of a single subject. The demarcation is purely for convenience and the two elements are closely intertwined, as we shall see.

II. BASIC CHARACTERISTICS OF FORMAL RULES

The term 'formal rules' has so far been used without defining it. Formal rules in the sense that the word is being used here have four basic features:

(1) Formal rules are intended to affect human behaviour, by influencing choice in decision situations. Needless to say, that intention may not actually be realized. It may even be recognized that a rule is no more than a symbol of what is approved or disapproved by authority rather than something that is really expected to be generally obeyed. All the same, formal rules normally have purposes other than their own existence. Gottlieb (1968, pp. 62, 111) makes the point by taking a cartoon depicting a sign in a boating pond which reads 'Do not tie boats to sign'. Such a rule strikes us as bizarre

precisely because it has no purpose other than its own existence.

(2) Formal rules are explicit statements conveying command, prohibition or permission and laying down the conditions to which those commands, prohibitions or permissions apply. A formal rule can be thought of as a sentence with a descriptive 'if . . . ' clause or protasis (for instance, 'In case of fire . . . ') and a prescriptive 'then . . . ' clause or apodosis (' . . . do not use lift') (see Twining and Miers, 1976, pp. 52–3).

(3) Formal rules embody at least some minimal amount of generality and universality. At least in principle, they apply to a group of cases. That is, rule protases (the descriptive 'if . . . ' clause) tend to be broader in scope than the expected facts of any individual case. A prescription or command specifically governing a unique event and addressed only to a single individual ('Leave this house!') is not a formal rule. (See Allott, 1980, p. 21.)

(4) Formal rules are designed and can in principle be changed. They are social management tools, not just generalizations about behaviour. Most of the time 'human nature', tastes and preferences, physical laws, have to be taken as given. But rules can be altered. Most, if not all, administrative analysis is ultimately about how people react to rules and how changes in rules might relate to changes in behaviour.

Each of these characteristics sets off a round of analytic problems which are familiar to those who make a profession of rule analysis, such as lawyers or philosophers. Some of these problems will be sketched out in later sections.

III. ADMINISTRATION BY 'RULE AND ROTE'

One well-known school of thought sees formal rules as not just unavoidable in the provision of public services, but positively desirable. The aim, it is held, should be to reduce *all* administration to 'rule and rote'. Administration should be like chess, or some similar board game, which is governed – indeed defined – by explicit rules which cover all conceivable situations which may arise and which admit of no ambiguity in their interpretation. What it should *not* be like, to this way of thinking, is the famous croquet game in *Alice in Wonderland.* In that case, the rules were arbitrarily made up and interpreted by one of the players, and changed from one minute to another, so that none of the other players knew what the rules were at any particular moment (Allott, 1980, p. 256, likens this to the USSR's penal law system). Many eighteenth-century thinkers wanted to approximate as closely as is ever possible to the famous slogan of 'a government of laws and not of men' (Article XXX of the 1780 Massachusetts Constitution). Exactly the same attitudes can be found today in (for instance) the 'welfare rights' movement, the movement for strict and non-discretionary business regulation, liberal arguments for national industrial policies based on clear rules articulated in advance rather than '*adhocery*', and so on.

If we wanted to reduce all public administration to 'rule and rote', following this school of thought, at least six features would need to be designed into the rule structure:

(1)   The rules must be knowable, discoverable by participants before they make the decisions which the rules govern. There should be no mystery about what the rules are.

(2)   The purpose served by the rules should be broadly acceptable and easy to see. Moreover, the rules should in fact serve the purpose for which they are intended – that is, they should incorporate valid cause–effect assumptions.

(3)   The rules must be completely consistent with one another, so as to avoid uncertainties bound up in 'umpiring' decisions about which rule gets priority in conflict-of-rule cases.

(4)   The protases of the rules (that is, the conditions in which the rules apply) should be completely specified in advance, to limit uncertainty as to when or where the rules apply.

(5)   Standards incorporated into rules should be capable of clear verification, so as to limit the scope for subjective interpretation.

(6)   Where rules divide behaviour or other items into

categories, those categories should be robust and unambiguous. ،

The rules of chess meet all of these conditions. The rules of Alice's croquet game meet none of them. The greater the extent to which a rule structure for public service provision can be made to possess these properties, the less will be the scope for 'arbitrary' rule interpretation. You could in principle substitute computers or robots for judges or enforcement agents. Enforcement might be a problem (a chess player can cheat, make mistakes or not know the rules in the first place), but rule interpretation would not be.

The sections which follow explore some of the practical difficulties of placing public service provision on the basis of a set of rules resembling those of chess, such that the job of enforcement and interpretation is potentially 'robotizable'. At the end of the chapter, we shall go back to the question of whether it is desirable even to try to put public services on such a 'laws not men' footing.

IV. RULE OPENNESS AND KNOWABILITY

The first requirement of a 'laws not men' approach to public service provision is that the rules should be knowable. Like the rules of chess, they should be transparent and easily accessible to the 'players' before they decide on their moves. But rule knowability can be frustrated in at least three ways: rules may be obscure; they may be unstable; or they may be deliberately concealed.

First, obscurity. For obscurity to be completely avoided (a) all the rules in the relevant rule structure must be set down in one place. Codification of rules – as in the Roman Law of the Twelve Tables, Justinian's Code, the Napoleonic Code Civil – is one important step towards knowability. And (b) the rules must be expressed in relatively simple 'idiot-proof' language so that they can be understood without extensive case law knowledge and statutory interpretation expertise. In other words, how simple it is to get to know the rules depends on whether those rules are written down, codified or indexed; on the plainness, opacity or ambiguity of the words in which they are framed; and on their complexity, in terms of the number of exceptions, special provisions, legal fictions, implicit presumptions, and the like which they contain.

The rules of chess meet both conditions (a) and (b) above. The US Constitution meets condition (a) but not condition (b). Equally, it is possible for rules to be simple to understand but unwritten or uncodified (as might apply, for instance, to the rules of a game played by children).

Second, stability. It will be easier for the 'players' to know what the rules are if those rules change infrequently or not at all. The rules of chess again meet this condition, but many rules governing social behaviour do not. If the rules are continually altered with changes in circumstances or on the whims of whoever makes the rules, it will be hard even for someone who wants to be law-abiding to be quite certain whether he is really obeying the rules or whether he has an enforceable claim under the rules. In some cases (decrees issued under a martial law regime, say) this may be very problematic. Allott (1980, p. 244) describes the case of a military governor of Northern Nigeria who made and changed laws in a way that could only be discovered by listening to radio broadcasts, thus compounding frequent change with lack of access to a complete set of written rules.

Even if rules are obscure and unstable, it may still be possible (if hard) to find out what the rules are. It can in principle be done if you pay the cost in time, trouble and expense to track down the rules. But even that may be impossible if rules are deliberately concealed by those who make them. Of course, this does not normally happen in chess. But some rules may become *arcanae imperii*, actively kept secret as a matter of strategy. Usually this occurs in circumstances where those subject to the rules are highly opportunistic, or are seen to be. For instance, office rules for tax law enforcement or eligibility to welfare benefits may not be revealed in detail for this reason. What amounts to the same thing, detailed reasons may not be given for taking action, if to do so might enable the ruled to infer what the rules being applied must be, and act accordingly. Obviously, such a practice is highly paternalistic, since the rules have to be taken on trust. But it does not necessarily always spring from motives of malevolence, self-interest or tyranny.

This sometimes happens with rules for allocating items in very high demand – such as titles and honours, examination grading, recruitment and promotion to prestigious posts. The exact criteria and reasons for decisions on such matters are often not revealed. The same sometimes happens to rules for enforcement, such as rules for prosecuting shoplifters by department store. Those to whom such rules apply may not be able, except by devious means, to find out exactly what the rules are. A variant is to present rules for public consumption which are different from the real rules. For instance, enforcement rules are often presented as more stringent than they really are. A store may declare in large-print notices that it always prosecutes shoplifters, but the actual rule may be not to prosecute people over 75 for trivial offences. A utility company may say that it cuts off supply to defaulting customers after 14 days, when the real rule is 28 days after the third warning.

Indeed, the 'board game' degree of rule accessibility is sometimes approached, but seldom reached, by real-life administrative rules. As was suggested earlier, it must not be supposed that failure to meet these conditions of knowability is always to be put down to turpitude or self-interest on the part of rule-makers. There may sometimes be plausible, even persuasive, reasons for departing from 100 per cent knowability. For instance, complexity and technical language in the framing of rules may bring precision even if they make the rules incomprehensible to the man in the street. Legal fictions are argued by some to be a matter of convenience and economy rather than deliberate obscurantism. Frequent change in rules may reflect desires to keep up to date, even to reflect changing popular opinion, rather than a tyrant's caprice. In circumstances where those to whom the rules apply are highly opportunistic, it may be tempting not to publicize the 'office rules'.

Consequences of Knowability

What difference does it make whether rules are 'knowable' or not? It can make a difference in at least three ways.

First, and most obviously, knowability affects the extent to which the layman can handle the rules for himself. Completely knowable and transparent rules in principle dispense with the need for a rule specialist, intermediary or 'lawyer'. Only the rawest of beginners at chess will need someone at his side to tell him what the rules are as he considers his moves, and even that can easily be dispensed with by reading the rules for himself. But where rules are obscure or unstable, the layman will need help from specialists, who invest time and money in mastering the rules. And where rules are not just obscure but deliberately kept secret, the only such rule specialists can be those who make and apply the rules – to the extent that such secrecy is effective, of course.

Second, rule knowability will affect the extent to which decisions made under the rules are capable of easy challenge or clear validation. Where rules are fully knowable and transparent, both challenge and validation becomes relatively easy. It is simply a matter of pointing to the relevant rule, as in chess. Where rules are obscure or scattered, challenging or demonstrating the validity of decisions made under them becomes laborious and expensive. But where rules are actively kept secret, challenging of decisions made under the rules becomes almost impossible and likewise the validity of those decisions can only be asserted, not demonstrated for all to see.

Third, knowability will affect the extent to which voluntary compliance with the rules is possible. Rules can normally be expected to change behaviour only if they are public and knowable in advance. Where rules are clear and easily accessible, failure to comply is more likely to reflect deliberate choice than ignorance or inability to invest in the requisite knowledge. Where rules are scattered or obscure, non-compliance will not necessarily reflect opportunism. 'Lloyds was a world of unwritten rules,' said the chief executive of the Lloyds insurance exchange after Lloyds had been rocked by a set of scandals in the 1970s, 'People were not obeying the unwritten rules because they didn't know what they were' (*Sunday Times*, 17 June 1984, p. 67). In such circumstances, compliance requires investment in mastering those rules, either directly or through using a specialist (or through the activity of enforcement agents, as we shall see in the next chapter). Where rules are actively kept secret, one can hardly obey the rules except by accident.

Accordingly, where there is (a) little opportunism; and (b) rules impose general duties or obligations, compliance will be made easier if the rules are kept simple, transparent, accessible in their entirety. (Of course, this will not stop those who disagree with the rules on principle from breaking them.) But where there is (a) a high degree of opportunism; and (b) rules convey opportunities and privileges rather than duties and obligations (for instance where they govern the allocation of highly-valued and scarce items) 'compliance' reasons for making the rules knowable hardly apply. In that case, it will be in the interest of those opportunists pursuing the benefits to master the rules. Indeed, they may well do so even if attempts are made to keep the rules secret.

In between those two extremes are a range of intermediate cases. For instance

(i)   Where opportunism is coupled with rules imposing obligations. Knowability will not necessarily reduce evasion by opportunists in that case.
(ii) Where lack of opportunism is coupled with rules conveying benefits or opportunities. Without knowability, there is insufficient opportunism for those affected to take up their rights.
(iii) Where rules govern neither general duties nor scarce benefits but regulate the assignment of costs or risks, such that they involve both opportunities and obligations.

V. RATIONALE AND CAUSAL VALIDITY

The second prerequisite for reducing public service provision to 'rule and rote' was that the rules should have a clear and generally acceptable rationale and that they should rest upon causally valid assumptions. Rules very often incorporate factual assumptions about relationships between cause and effect (for instance, between the presence of alcohol and crowd violence in football grounds) and the efficacy of rules can turn on the correctness of those cause-effect assumptions.

(1) Basic Underlying Rationale

If a rule structure rests upon a clear rationale:

- (a) the reason for the rules is easy to see; and
- (b) Once one grasps a few basic principles, it is possible to work out what the rules are likely to be in any particular case.

For instance, since a seminal article by Coase (1960, pp. 1–44) on the English common–law doctrine of 'reasonable use' in nuisance or incompatible joint-use cases, writers on the economics of law have argued that many of the liability rules of the common law can be seen as ways of promoting efficient allocation of resources. They are said, for instance, to follow a principle of encouraging voluntary exchange where transactions costs are low, and of assigning liability to risk to whichever party runs the least cost in bearing the risk. In this vein, Posner (1977, p. 178) asserts that

> the common law exhibits a deep unity that is economic in character . . . The common-law method is to allocate responsibilities between interacting activities in such a way as to maximize the joint value or, what amounts to the same thing, minimize the joint cost of their activities. It may do this by redefining a property right, by devising a new rule of liability or by recognizing a contract right

Posner argues that the same can be said of the rules governing remedies, such as the way that compensatory damages are fixed or the preference for the award of lump-sum damages rather than periodic payments to injured parties (to encourage them, if possible, to overcome the effects of the damage sustained as quickly as they can, as well as saving on administrative costs).

We noted earlier (section II) that formal rules are framed for some purpose other than their own existence. But a rule structure may well have a discoverable underlying rationale even if the original designers had no very clear idea of the general purposes they were pursuing at the time when the rules were drawn up. For instance, the common law liability rules originally developed in the light of a vague and semi-articulate sense of 'fairness' rather than the elaborate economic theory justification for them offered by writers like Posner.

Contrariwise, the passage of time may obscure what was originally the clear purpose of a rule, or make that purpose obsolete. This often accounts for the apparently senseless rules which we come across in ancient institutions. Or a rule may have a general rationale but yet make no sense in a particular context, as with those US safety regulations in the 1970s requiring that arthritis pills be sold in childproof containers which arthritic people were unlikely to be able to open (Macrae, 1984, pp. 114–15). Or again, piecemeal accretions to the rules from diverse sources may mean that the structure as a whole lacks any clear underlying rationale which, once mastered, causes everything to fall into place, as it were. For instance, no equivalent to the general rationale claimed by writers such as Posner to underly much of the common law can be found in the case of the statute law in general or of administrative law in the common law countries.

To the extent to which a rule structure possesses a clear underlying rationale, it means;

(a) Knowability of the rules should be enhanced (if they all follow some general philosophy).
(b) Compliance with the rules should be enhanced, provided that the basic purpose of the rules is acceptable to those to whom the rules apply.
(c) A basis can exist for 'rational' criticism of the rules, in the sense of scope for showing some of the rules to be illogical, anomalous or obsolescent in terms of that underlying rationale. A classic example is Adam Smith's argument that eighteenth-century property succession rules (entail, primogeniture) hampered rather than promoted the development of real estate, since landowners under such rules had little incentive or capacity to develop their properties to the fullest possible extent (Smith, 1978, pp. 64–7, 70–1).

Valid Cause-and-Effect Assumptions

Rules may have a clear and generally acceptable rationale and yet embody false assumptions about cause and effect. For instance, the US Securities and Exchange Act 1933 had an obvious and fairly unexceptionable rationale – to protect the innocent investor from unscrupulous operators. But was it correct to assume that registration of stock dealers and disclosure rules governing new stock issues would serve to improve the lot of investors? Not according to a controversial study by Stigler (1964, pp. 117–42), which showed that investors in common stocks in the 1950s fared no better on average than their counterparts of the 1920s if they held the securities for less than two years.

If public services are to be a matter of 'laws not men', and all latitude for human judgement in interpretation or enforcement is to be removed, a great deal of effort, time and expense must be put into researching the cause-and-effect relationships in the situations which are to be regulated. This is, of course, very difficult. Every day, rules come under attack on the ground that they do not in fact realize their intended purposes – however benevolent or generally acceptable those purposes may be – because they are built on false causal assumptions. For instance, is it correct to assume (as the first 'social engineers' of Imperial Rome did) that the way to increase the incidence of marriage and child-rearing is to restrict the capacity of unmarried or childless adults to benefit under a will? (See Allott, 1980, p. 77.) Or that a rule prescribing heavy mandatory penalties for some offence will reduce the incidence of that offence, rather than making courts reluctant to convict and informers to inform? Will banning such and such a food additive or pesticide really reduce the incidence of cancer? Will a rule obliging monoglot English-speaking college students to spend vacations in minority-language areas help to strengthen the status of the minority language by causing everybody to learn it, or further weaken the minority language as a result of the influx of English-speakers?

Testing questions such as these to the 'beyond a reasonable doubt' level of proof required for conviction in a criminal trial is typically either impossible or inordinately expensive. Breyer (1982, pp. 138–9) makes the point in relation to food additives regulation, citing a report by a leading group of US scientists who asserted that to be able to say with 0.999 confidence that a given substance was not toxic would require negative results on 3 million laboratory test animals. Majone (in Weiss and Barton 1980, p. 246) gives an even more extreme case.

The lazy way out of this kind of problem is to adopt a preponderance of the evidence standard rather than a proof beyond a reasonable doubt standard in establishing cause-and-effect relationships on which the rules bear. Then uncertainty can be coped with by:

(a)   changing the rules whenever the underlying cause-and-effect assumptions start to look doubtful;
(b)   bending the rules by changing the way that they are interpreted, either from time to time, or from case to case;
(c)   selectively enforcing the rules, such that they do not in practice apply in circumstances where their underlying assumptions seem problematic.

But coping with uncertainty in rule-making by these means goes wholly against the spirit of a 'laws not men' approach to public service provision. Changing the rules from one moment to the next potentially removes the 'knowability' condition. Selective enforcement or discretionary interpretation are precisely what the 'laws not men' approach is trying to get away from. To stand by that approach requires rule-makers to undertake the burden of amassing all the relevant information, and ultra-rigorous testing of the causal relationships assumed by a proposed rule in advance of its enactment. To do so in all cases is to tax knowledge and rationality to its limits, let alone time and resources.

VI. ABSENCE OF CONTRADICTION

A third requirement of a 'laws not men' approach to public service provision, as we saw earlier, is that no rules should contradict other rules (or contradict themselves, as in: 'The rule is, jam yesterday and jam tomorrow, but never jam today'). Consistency obviously relates to rationale, since a body of contradictory rules cannot have a clear overall rationale.

In board games such as chess the rules are perfectly consistent with one another. And 'the law' is likewise assumed to be a completely unified, self-consistent body of rules comparable to the rules of chess. But this is of course a fiction (albeit an important one), not a literal description. Conflicts between administrative rules are commonplace. The phrase 'Catch 22' has entered the language to denote those situations in which one rule effectively negates another. Rule conflicts, then, logically require other rules to deal with the handling of clashes. Of course, those second-stage rules might themselves conflict, and so on.

A set of rules may be inconsistent for at least four reasons. First, and perhaps simplest, situations so 'odd' that no one foresaw them, may suddenly crop up and reveal potential conflicts between the rules. Suppose you go to a public park for a picnic. Notices tell you not to drop litter and to keep off the grass. Obediently, you settle on a bench just off the greensward and carefully collect the debris of your picnic in a bag. Suddenly, a freak, unforeseeable gust of wind snatches up the rubbish bag, depositing its contents all over the grass. What do you do? Through no fault of your own, you have got into a situation where you can only follow one of the park rules by breaking the other one.

Second, contradictions may develop because rules embody rival principles amongst which we genuinely cannot decide 'once and for all'. The rule that trespassers on land cannot complain of harm that they suffer there rubs up against the rule that landowners have a duty to protect those who come onto their land when the intruders are unaware of the danger they are in (cf. Posner, 1977, pp. 128–31; Allott, 1980 p. 57, 101–3). Probably the most striking example is the rules for interpreting statutes and using precedents in common law countries, where opposing canons can be found for almost every point, for instance where literal reading of the rules leads to anomalous results.

Third, rules may come into conflict because they are made or operated by different or rival institutions. It is far from uncommon to find oneself in a situation where the rules of institution A require you to complete a transaction with institution B before you can complete a related transaction with A (for instance, in completing various linked parts of a real estate deal, such as making an offer, obtaining mortgage funds, obtaining possession or building clearance). At the same time, institution B's rules require you to complete the necessary transaction with A before you can close with B ... As legal systems develop, it is common to find outright conflict in the rules operated by various courts and bodies of law. The development of equity law and canon law (in matters such as the enforcement of contracts and the regulation of testamentary succession) alongside the common law in European countries in early modern times is a case in point.

Fourth, and much less innocently, contradictory rules may be tolerated or even deliberately designed so that those who adjudicate or decide the balance between contradictory rules will be able to swing their weight in one direction or another, and to reverse direction at will. This, of course, is what judges do when they put their weight behind one rather than another of the contradictory canons of interpretation which might apply to a particular statute or precedent. It is precisely because they have contradictory rules or legal principles 'up their sleeve' that they can adapt their decisions to whatever seem to be the needs of the moment – for instance, on whether it seems at the time of judgement that (as in our park example) it is more important to crack down in littering or to protect the grass. In Chapter 4, we shall look at the use of contradictory rules as a means for superordinates to exert control over their underlings in large-scale employment enterprises.

The more standards or desiderata that a rule structure embodies, the more likely it is that those standards or desiderata will conflict with one another. This happens too often in the rules for business regulation to be put down to accident or lack of foresight rather than to design. Breyer (1982, pp. 78–9) cites the extreme case of the US Federal Communications Commission, which until 1965 operated under rules specifying 14 different criteria which were to govern its allocation of broadcasting licences to TV stations. He comments, 'The effect of many standards . . . is virtually the same as having none at all. . . . The existence of so many standards effectively allows the agency near-total discretion in making a selection.'

For one or all of these reasons, formal rule structures often seem to follow a variant of Newton's third law of motion. That is, for every rule there tends to grow up an equal and opposite rule. This is not a problem if one is prepared to allow judges, administrators, enforcement agents, some latitude in deciding which rule gets priority in the many cases where rules come into conflict. But again, that 'lazy' way out of the difficulty will not satisfy us if we are bent on a 'laws not men' approach to public service provision. All possible contingencies where rules might conflict must then be foreseen and provided for in advance. Rival principles must be ranked once and for all, rather than balanced against one another as events unfold. The potentially control-enhancing effects of cross-cutting contradictory rules must certainly be quite foresworn. The difficulties of following such a programme in practice are easy to see.

VII. SPECIFICATION OF RULE PROTASES

We saw earlier that formal rules may be thought of as 'if . . . then' sentences. The 'if . . . ' clause, or protasis, gives the conditions in which the rule applies. We also saw that a 'laws not men' approach to public service provision would require the conditions in which each rule applies to be comprehensively specified.

Again, the rules of chess fully satisfy this condition. But once one goes outside the world of board games, the protases of most real-life rules can never be completely specified. To do so would require an omniscient rule-designer capable of anticipating all the possible combinations of circumstances which might conceivably bear on the rule, including developments or inventions which do not exist now but might do so in the future (see Hart, 1961, p. 123).

Most formal rules designed to regulate human behaviour have some degree of uncertainty or incompleteness in the specification of their 'if . . . ' clause. A standard example used by academic lawyers to demonstrate the point is a rule forbidding vehicles in a public park (Hart, 1961, pp. 123–6; Gottlieb, 1968, pp. 45, 108, 113; Twining and Miers, 1976, pp. 118–19, 122, 240–2). For instance, would such a rule invalidate the erection of a monument involving a vehicle (say, as a war memorial)? Could it be invoked by a policeman to block the entrance of an ambulance rushing to the scene of an injured child in the park?

Ordinarily, such nit-picking considerations are quite out of place for rules like this. Given goodwill on all sides and a reasonable understanding of the purpose of the rule, few 'hard cases' will arise. Ordinarily, it would be ridiculous for the 'no vehicles' notice to specify the rule's protases in detail, by discussing the erection of monuments, and the like.

It is just when that condition is absent that rule protases will become most problematic. For instance, such a situation might occur if a campaigning group were seeking to discredit the park's rules by deliberately contriving 'hard cases'. In those conditions, as has been noted, ever more detailed specification of the rule's protasis will be required. And of course, a commitment to a 'laws not men' approach in any case implies rejection on principle of any reliance on goodwill and common sense to make the rules work in practice.

VIII. OBJECTIVE STANDARDS

A rule's protasis may refer to standards of behaviour which is required or disfavoured. For instance, a rule based on the cause–effect assumption that worn tyres cause accidents may specify that owners of vehicles with tyres below a stipulated tread depth are liable to punishment.

In order to limit uncertainty and scope for varying interpretation or enforcement, the 'laws not men' approach demands that such standards be fully worked out, clear and objectively verifiable. For instance, if a rule says that unsafe buildings must be demolished, the standard of safety must be fully and objectively specified.

Obviously, this condition is easier to satisfy in some cases than in others. For instance, it is easier to set down objectifiable conditions for condemning dangerous automobiles than for condemning dangerous buildings. The former process lends itself, in principle at least, to replicable testing and precise measurement, in relation to matters such as tyre tread depth or coefficient of braking efficiency. But buildings are much harder to 'test' (except by destruction) and have a much greater degree of uniqueness (due to varying subsoil conditions) than automobiles.

All that can be done in the latter type of case is to employ a standard which is objectively verifiable in *procedural* terms – for instance, that two qualified building surveyors must independently inspect a building before it is certified as dangerous, or that the demolition order must be issued by a magistrate (see Majone, in Weiss and Barton, 1980, pp. 235–58). Indeed, long ago, Griffith and Street (1952, p. 147) argued that the emergence of loosely-framed, procedurally specified standards rather than objectifiable substantively-framed ones was a hallmark of a developed legal system. The problem, of course, with relying on rigorous procedures rather than on substantive standards for condemnation of dangerous buildings and the like is that the procedures may be too cumbersome in certain circumstances – for instance, when an emergency situation develops suddenly in a building in a remote area.

Standards which cannot be objectively specified may work well enough in practice in some conditions. Things may go smoothly enough if there is goodwill on all sides, a general disposition to trust 'expert' judgement, general agreement on what counts as relevant expertise and general agreement among the experts themselves. But what if these cosy conditions do not apply? What if one construction expert declares that the cracks in a building only indicate normal settlement and that the edifice is sound for 50 years, but another expert interprets those cracks as presaging imminent collapse? Such differences are by no means rare. Even if problems of that kind never appeared, a procedurally defined rather than substantively defined standard represents a distinct watering down of the 'objectifiability' standard implied in a strict 'laws not men' approach.

IX. ROBUST RULE CATEGORIES

Often, the protasis of a rule involves multiple categories, with the apodosis depending on what category a case falls in. This happens, for instance, where the amount of income taken in tax depends on the income bracket or personal circumstances category of the taxpayer, or where the degree of care required depends on the category in which a person is placed (for instance, blind versus sighted persons). The last requirement of a 'laws not men' approach to framing rules for public service provision is that the categories into which a rule divides the world to which it relates should be unambiguous and robust. This too, is easier to prescribe than to achieve in practice.

(1) Unambiguous Specification

Some categories are perhaps more inherently vague than others – for instance, where we are dealing with highly abstract distinctions remote from most people's daily experience (Allott, 1980, pp. 34–6). And some, perhaps much, ambiguity in categorization may spring from ineptitude, carelessness or avoidable lack of foresight. For instance (to take a case that once did arise in charity law), if 'young persons under 21 and unmarried' are to be eligible for some benefit, it must not be left in doubt whether that 'and' is conjunctive (= 'both . . . and') or disjunctive (= 'either . . . or'). Obviously, all such avoidable vagueness in categorization must be eliminated if the 'laws not men' approach is to be realized.

But categorization can be problematic even for apparently down-to-earth matters and where the rules are framed with all available skill and experience. For instance, pre-nineteenth century protectionist economic policy required that all ships coming into British ports be classed as 'native' or 'foreign'. This involved, over the century ending in the Act of General Registry 1786, a long process of refinement and running repairs to these categories (Jarvis, 1973). The categories had to reflect the fine-grained and changing nature of the constitutional relationships among the British group of countries, for instance in respect of Scotland and the Isle of Man. They also had to accommodate all the various possible dimensions of 'nativeness' and 'foreign-ness' – for instance, ships which were part home-built and part foreign-built, part home-owned and part foreign-owned, part home-manned and part foreign-manned, and all the various possible permutations of 'hybrid' and 'pure' characteristics in these three dimensions.

The problem, in part at least, reflects the inherent imprecision and contextual definition of terms used in natural language. As Fuller (1967, p. 102) puts it, 'Natural' classes rarely, if ever, exist. We are constantly encountering borderline cases which upset our classifications. . . . Even those qualities which seem so opposed that they are used as synonyms for the idea of contrast – black and white, life and death – shade into one another by imperceptible degrees.' The jurists' favourite example of the 'no vehicles in the park' rule, as mentioned earlier, can be used to generate obvious potential ambiguities about what is to count as a 'vehicle'. Wheelchairs? Shopping baskets on wheels? Prams? Toy vehicles? Sledges? Horses? Sedan chairs? Stretchers?

Hence, the more that is at stake and the more that interests conflict, the more pressure rule categories will be subjected to, even if those categories do not seem to deal with matters of inherent ambiguity. Every commentator on legal theory brings this point out in one way or another. It is now a commonplace that the meaning of rules expressed in general terms is 'socially constructed' rather than automatically drawable from a literal reading of the words in which the rule is expressed (unlike rules expressed in artificial languages such as algebra or computer language). Kagan (1978, pp. 88–90) provides a useful short summary of 'social construction of meaning' in the context of formal rules. He says (ibid., p. 89) 'the use of rules is . . . a social process, in which participants draw on a learned repertoire of conventions to produce shared understandings of what the rules mean and when they should be applied'. The more opportunism or conflict of interest that operates on the rules, the less reliance can be placed on generally specified rules which are commonly understood to possess a particular meaning. If rule meaning is subject to social construction, it is also subject to opportunistic destruction.

Obviously, too, that linguistic pressure on the rule categories will tend to be greater, and the more 'manufactured' category ambiguity will appear, the more stark is the transition from one category to another and the more that is at stake in whether a particular case falls into one category or another (Hood 1976, pp. 60–70). For example, Kagan (1978, p. 135) describes the operation of a 90-day price freeze in the USA in 1971. In such a case, major interests hang on how particular items or activities are categorized, and predictably Kagan reports many vexing categorization problems. For instance, was a reduction in service to be categorized as an increase in price? Examples of contrived category ambiguity which are current at the time of writing include cases making problematic the borderline between underwear and food (must flavoured underwear comply with food regulations?), and the borderline between serviceable and scrap automobiles (Is a brand-new car which is sawn in half before importation to a country, to be welded together afterwards, to count as scrap for the purposes of customs duty?)

Such borderline categorization problems are hard to avoid completely at the best of times. They reach an extreme point where there are only two possible categories, and momentous consequences hang on whether any given case is classed into one or another – for instance, when one's result in an important test or exam can only be classed as 'pass' or 'fail', when the verdict in a murder trial can only be 'guilty' or 'not guilty'; when one can only be classed 'fit' or 'unfit' for work. We can expect in those circumstances a pile of troublesome 'borderline' cases, as in that awkward boundary-line between the nearly but not quite disabled and the just but only just disabled (see Mashaw, 1983, p. 93).

(2) Robustness of Categories

Closely related to ambiguity is the robustness of the categories built into a rule. To be robust, a rule's categories must correspond to clear-cut break-points or fault-lines in the actual arrangement of the world to be categorized rather than cutting across them. Category robustness is another requirement of the 'laws not men' approach to rule-making.

Figure 2.1 is an exaggerated example of the robustness problem (it builds on Dunsire, 1980, pp. 40–2). It shows two hypothetical sets of test scores under a rule which provides for a test of quality. The precise subject of the test does not matter. It might be a quality-control test on a product (say, meat or water), or a proficiency test for a skill (say, flying a plane or driving a truck). Suppose:

(a) The cases to be examined are graded by testers on a judgemental scale running from 0–100.
(b) Several testers are used for the job, with standards of judgement that vary a little from one tester to another, and even the same tester's absolute judgement may be subject to some uncertainty and inconsistency over

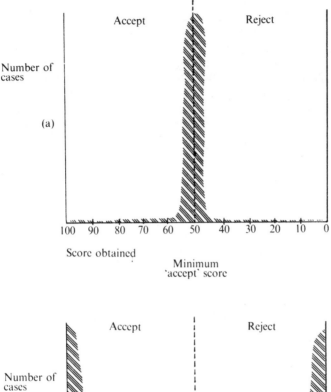

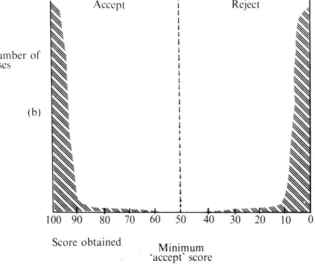

Figure 2.1   Category robustness: quality testing

multiple cases. Suppose that the zone of uncertainty in grading judgements for these reasons is 5 per cent, above or below the score actually given.

(c) Each case to be tested must go into one of only two categories – accept (pass) or reject (fail). Those which are graded 50 or more are accepted, while those graded below 50 are rejected.

If the cases arrange themselves as in Figure 2.1(a), the categories are anything but robust. It is a quality tester's nightmare. Virtually all of the test cases turn out to be graded within the range 46–54. Given the 5 per cent uncertainty zone, the categorization of all of these cases is potentially problematic. Every case graded 'reject' might be graded 'accept' by a different tester or by the same tester on another occasion, and vice versa. If the testers in such a case want to increase the robustness of categorization, they must:

(a) change the boundary-line between accept and reject – say, to a score of 60 or 40 – so that all those much of a muchness cases graded in the range 46–54 go into the same category; *or*

(b) find another way of testing the cases which will not result in them all bunching tightly around the accept/reject line; *or*

(c) try to cut down the zone of uncertainty in the testers' grading – for instance, by objective testing rather than judgemental scaling.

But if the cases arrange themselves as in Figure 2.1(b), the categories are very robust – a quality tester's dream. There are no cases graded within the 'problem' range 46–54 and most cases are piled up either around a grade of 0 or a grade of 100. Even given the 5 per cent uncertainty zone in testers' judgement – indeed, even if that zone of uncertainty were much wider – there are no problem cases.

Obviously, the seriousness of this kind of problem will depend on what is at stake in the categorization and on whether there are opportunities for repeat testing. If the cases in Figure 2.1 are candidates in a beautiful baby or knobbly knees competition, the robustness problem may not be of much moment. If they are nuclear installations graded for acceptable safety standards, it is another matter. Similarly, the robustness problem is less serious if there are opportunities for repeat testing – for instance if having failed the proficiency test once, you can enter again later. But where retesting is inherently impossible (say, where products are highly perishable, like fresh fish, or where papers or items submitted for test can subsequently be destroyed), the robustness problem becomes more serious.

Even where retesting is impossible and where much is at stake in categorization, complete robustness cannot always be realized in categorization, for at least three reasons.

(1) There may simply *be* no clear break-points to be found in the relevant population. For instance, those quality-test cases in Figure 2.1(a) may still bunch tightly on the margin of acceptable quality whatever mode of testing is employed – by computers or humans, by a single tester or multiple testers, by judgemental or objective standards.

(2) The distribution of the break-points in the population may be potentially volatile, while the boundaries of the categories must remain constant over time for some reason. For instance, it might well be that the 'tester's dream' result of Figure 2.1(b) occurs on one batch of tests and the 'tester's nightmare' of figure 2.1(a) occurs on the next batch. In principle, the location of the boundary line between accept and reject might be moved to take care of the robustness problem, as mentioned above. But there may well be constraints other than mere inertia on altering rule categories over time in such a way. For instance, testers might well be required to maintain consistency of absolute judgement, competence levels and mode of testing over time, so that the acceptable quality level required of, say, meat offered for sale this week is expected to be the same as that required of the meat offered for sale last week.

(3) Opportunism. 'Pyramid selling' is a chain-selling process whereby people are recruited to earn commission on selling high-cost products directly to the public at home, with cash rewards for recruiting new recruits to the scheme, irrespective of whether those new distributors actually sell the product.

After its heyday in the early 1970s, pyramid selling is now illegal in many countries.

But pyramid selling has been succeeded by 'multi-level marketing' (MLM). MLM so closely resembles pyramid selling that the casual observer could scarcely tell the difference. But technically, MLM is not categorized as 'pyramid selling' in that distributors are not paid a cash bonus for each new recruit (as in pyramid selling) and do not *directly* obtain a share of the profit on goods sold by those specifically recruited by themselves. In MLM, the earlier you are recruited, the bigger the share you get of the *aggregated* sales achieved by all later recruits (cf. Levene, 1983, p. 63). Artifice has created a class of activity just, but only just, outside the forbidden category of 'pyramid selling'.

This is just one example of the way that opportunistic behaviour tends to pile up cases near the borderlines, even if those borderlines are originally fixed at clear-cut break-points. To avoid that problem, categories must rest on characteristics which it is not possible to change by artifice – for instance, where you were born, rather than where you choose to live now, seniority or first come first served rather than merit or need (even the seniority principle requires a tie-break rule, of course). But the problem of achieving category robustness by such means is obvious enough. First, the inherent possibilities of categorizing human beings in this way are limited. Even physical appearance can be greatly modified, if the stakes are high enough. Second, categorization which meets this criterion tends to go to accidents of history or genealogy rather than to current characteristics, and this runs up rather sharply against modern ideas of equity and social engineering.

Even if rule categories are robust against the kind of problems constituted by (1) and (2) above, the threat posed to robustness by (3) – opportunism – can rarely be eliminated entirely. In practice, as we shall see in the next chapter, this problem is often dealt with by public bureaucracies selectively enforcing over-inclusive rules rather than by trying to frame ultra-precise rules in the first place (on this point, see Posner, 1977, p. 424; Veljanovski, in Hawkins and Thomas, 1984, pp. 173–5). But that, of course, goes completely against the spirit of the 'laws not men' approach.

X. SUMMARY AND CONCLUSION

(1) The Limits of the 'Laws not Men' Approach

Sections IV–IX have shown some of the difficulties of putting public service provision on the same footing as a game of chess – that is, to order it strictly within a set of objective, given, mechanically applicable rules. At most, that can only be an ideal to be approached or a yardstick against which to set actual rules rather than a scheme which can ever be fully realized. Each of the six preconditions of a 'laws not men' approach, as listed in section III, is a severe test of the rule-maker's foresight and capacity to provide for all relevant conditions. The odds against meeting any of those conditions in full in rules governing public services are high. The odds against meeting all of those conditions simultaneously in any set of real-world rules are very high.

These six conditions overlap considerably and, as we saw, meeting one will often go towards meeting another (for instance, clear rationale and absence of contradiction will tend to promote knowability of the rules). But there are also potential incompatibilities between them, such that one can get closer to one condition only by giving ground on another. For instance, categories can be made very robust if based on features which are difficult for opportunists to change – such as age, place of birth, grandfather's occupation. But it is likely to be hard to give a clear rationale for using only categories of that kind. Similarly, elaboration of rule protases to cover every eventuality, or minute specification of standards, will run the risk of reducing knowability, making the rules incomprehensible to the layman. (Kelman, in Hawkins and Thomas, 1984, p. 103, points out this dilemma in the framing of US occupational and safety rules.)

Some would even reject the 'laws not men' approach as a desirable ideal. It might be held to hinder rapid adaptation, either to the strategies of opportunists or to other types of new contexts. Given a changing context and a limited capacity to comprehend even the causal connections in the existing environment (let alone to predict all possible future contingencies), there may be good reasons for not completely or unambiguously specifying rule protases, standards, categories. A degree of ambiguity, uncertainty, even outright contradiction, can allow some play for judgement and discretion, so that rules can be adapted by varying interpretation as circumstances change. So argued Dr Johnson, observing, 'A country is in a bad state, which is governed only by laws; because a thousand things occur for which laws cannot provide, and where authority ought to interpose . . . ' (Boswell, 1909, p. 159).

(2) Differences between Board Game Rules and Administrative Rules

In fact, there are at least two important differences between rules in games like chess and rules governing public services. These differences have been pointed out by Gottlieb (1968, pp. 54–6). His argument is as follows.

First, we normally play games like chess in order to follow the rules of chess, since the game is defined only by the rules (which are themselves determinate and given). But this does not normally apply to public services. Of course, some administrative or public service rules are more chess-like than others. But we do not park a car just to follow rules about parking, nor build a house in order to follow rules about building. In the case of public services, the relevant activity tends to be constrained but not exactly and exhaustively constituted by the rules.

Second, where an activity is governed but not constituted and exhaustively defined by formal rules (as in parking as opposed to chess), Gottlieb argues that the protases of formal rules can never be comprehensive. There will always be the possibility of unforeseen circumstances throwing the application of the rules into doubt, or of 'material facts' other than those referred to in the protases of the rules.

This is very important for the opportunist. In chess, opportunism must either be exercised within the rules (by strategic skill in moving the pieces as the rules allow) or outside the rules (say, by 'psyching' your opponent). But in activities which are not defined by rules, opportunism can be *about* the formal rules as well as within or outside them. Taxpayers may treat the tax rules as part of the tax game, not as what defines that game. As we saw in sections VII–IX, even apparently quite straightforward and uncontroversial rules may give some scope for the opportunist exploiting the properties of natural language and incompletely specified rule protases.

Hence the significance of the social context in which the rules operate. If absolutely everyone has the same understanding of what the rules mean, quite sketchily or sloppily drafted, half-articulated rules may serve well enough. But where there is opportunism or no shared understanding of what the rules mean, the rule designer must try to provide for the possible moves of opportunists trying to get round the rules as well as to eliminate honest perplexity and anticipate all 'exogenous' contingencies which might arise. Obviously, this will add enormously to the cost, effort and intellectual rigour needed to frame the rules. Everything implicit must be ever more definitively spelled out; ever more contingencies foreseen and provided for; interpretation ever more minutely specified. The 'loophole industry' and 'counter-loophole industry' which develop around the rules for taxation or real-estate zoning are dramatic examples of what this can mean in practice.

(3) Rule Making and Rule Enforcement

The more we try to get towards the 'laws not men' conditions, the more difficult and costly the process of framing the rules becomes. But the more we depart from that condition, the more problematic it will be to enforce and interpret those rules. Rule making and rule enforcement then cease to be distinct activities. As we noted in section IX, some of the costs and effort of framing rules to meet 'laws not men' conditions can be limited by passing the problems into the sphere of enforcement activity. But at the same time as limiting the cost and effort of keeping the rules up-to-date and foreseeing every possible 'special case' contingency at the design stage, this necessarily increases the effort and uncertainty of enforcement.

But even if the rules of public service provision *could* be like the rules of chess in their comprehensiveness and unambiguity, they would still have to be enforced. Opportunists, who know and share the received interpretation of what the rules are, can still cheat at chess by secretly breaking the rules. Novices or incompetents can make mistakes because they don't know or can't remember what the rules are. Cranks or dissidents can dismiss the rules as silly and pointless and flout them in favour of their own version of what the rules of chess ought to be. The next chapter looks at the rule enforcement problem.

QUESTIONS FOR REVIEW

1. Suppose that a local flood control commission for V is to be established, as discussed in section I. Design a structure of rules for the operation of the commission, using the six categories of rules described in section I.

2. Suppose that the scope rule for the local flood commission reads as follows: 'The Commissioners shall have power to levy such taxes, requisition such property, perform such actions and enter into such transactions as they may think fit on any matter which in their opinion relates to flood defences in or near V.' Suppose that the commissioners use their powers of requisitioning property as the basis for entering the real-estate development business, on the grounds that speculative gains realized from land transactions will help to finance the commission's activities and keep their staff busy in slack times. How might the scope rule be redrafted to prevent such activities while still leaving the commissioners with draconian powers to cope with a real emergency?

3. You are responsible for collecting taxes in a community of intelligent and well-informed opportunists. You follow a rule of not prosecuting for late payment until six months after the due date, and not prosecuting for under-payment if it is below a specified sum. Ought these rules to be made public or not?

4. Can you think of possible uncertainty in the protasis of the rule saying which side of the road we should drive on?

5. It is the year 2000 AD. Big strides have taken place in personal robot technology. Some robots are set on wheels, others 'walk' on legs. Two robot owners, A and B, programme their robots to take their dogs for a walk in

Jurists' Park, at the entry to which is a large notice saying 'No Vehicles'. A's robot is wheeled, B's legged. Under the 'no vehicles' rule, would you allow entry to (a) both robots; (b) neither robot; (c) one robot but not the other? What do you think would hang upon such a decision?

GUIDE TO FURTHER READING

A good legal/philosophical analysis of formal rules, heavily drawn upon here, is Gottlieb (1968). The same goes for an excellent standard text by Twining and Miers (1976, esp. pp. 48–72, 110–28). Hart's (1961) treatment is more specifically set in an (English) legal context, but it is a classic exposition. Allott (1980) offers – mainly from a legal background – an account of the limits of formal rules as a 'policy lever' or autonomous instrument of social change. An analysis of rules which comes from the stable of game theory rather than law and philosophy is Ostrom (1984), which has also been drawn upon here. On the limitations of natural language for unambiguous rule formulation, see Hood (1976) and Kagan (1978), as well as the sources mentioned above.

3 Making it Stick: Enforceability Analysis

'. . . John Marshall has made his decision, now let him enforce it.' (Said to have been remarked by President Andrew Jackson of the US Supreme Court's judgment in *Worcester v. Georgia 1832* [Scigliano, 1971, p. 36].)

Making rules is one thing. Enforcing them is another. Part of the commonsense understanding of what administration is about is carrying out decisions or enforcing rules against potential resistance or evasion. And *public* administration, in so far as it involves the *public* power and services with *public* good features about them, is in large part about compelling people to do what they would not do voluntarily. We saw that in the flood-control story with which we began. Chapter 1 left V's story at the point at which the provision of two services basic to human existence could hardly be secured without some degree of compulsion in requiring payment and appropriation of land.

That, of course, is where the problems *start*, not where they end. What if people refuse to pay the compulsory levies for flood control? What if they artfully evade the tax by some stratagem or another? What if those whose property rights are to be overridden show defiance, barricading their land against intruders? These are not just far-fetched theoretical possibilities. The disposition to break rules, orders, decisions, agreements, may be more or less, depending on the circumstances. It may be expressed in open defiance or in concealed evasion. But it is rarely completely absent. Just as formal rules differ from physical laws and 'human nature' in that they are 'designable' (as we saw in the last chapter), they also differ in that they are evadable. Hence the enforcement problem – a central and traditional concern of administrative analysis.

Some Examples

Consider the following situations:

(1) A government bans strikes during a war or national emergency (or for some other reason). Then 50,000 key workers prepare to go on strike.

(2) Country A's authorities permit a merger between a domestic firm and a company based abroad on condition that the merged entity maintain its head office in A. Soon afterwards, the new company announces that for reasons 1, 2 ... n, it is moving its head office out of A.

(3) X, an influential member of a close-knit community, refuses to pay a tax to which he objects on principle. Tax officials set off the legal process of seizing his assets. His valuable furniture and stock are put up for auction in a saleroom in his local community. Mysteriously, only one individual (a close associate of X's) bids at the auction and buys the whole stock for a nominal sum, so that government receives nothing.

(4) Countries B and C each fish a lake which lies partly in B and partly in C. Because fish stocks are running low, B and C agree to take no more than 10,000 units of fish each out of the lake each year. In the first year of the agreement, scientific observers estimate that not less than 30,000 units of fish have been taken out of the lake.

(5) An association makes a rule that if any of its members win more than a stipulated sum of money on dice or cards or horse-racing, they must give the surplus over to the association's funds. Gambling goes on. No contributions are received.

(6) An offender Y, found guilty by a court, is ordered to pay a fine in 50 instalments. Y faithfully pays the first 40 instalments on the due dates, then maintains that unforeseen financial difficulties prevent him from making the remaining 10 payments in the given time.

(7) Z owns an old house without modern amenities (bath, WC, etc.). The house is officially scheduled as a building to be

preserved, so that Z may not alter the basic structure. Government's general policy is to encourage people to instal modern amenities in their houses and it gives money to help them to do so. Accordingly, Z decides to put a shower in his house. Official safety rules say that all showers of the type which Z wants to fit must incorporate a cold-water header tank. Because of the nature of Z's house (low roof and no loft, let us say) in the only place where it is practicable to fit the shower, the only way that Z can observe the header-tank rule is by altering the structure of the building, which he is forbidden to do under the preservation rule, (this is a conflict-of-rules problem such as we encountered in the last chapter). Exasperated, Z decides to instal his shower without the required header tank.

(8) An elderly lady is seen taking a dress out of a department store without payment. She seem confused and appears unable to speak the language of the country. Haltingly, she states that she is not used to department stores and was only taking the dress outside to look at it in the light. She says this is the custom where she comes from.

Question: What do you think should be done next in each of these situations?

Enforceability problems of the kind illustrated in these eight examples (each of which is related to a real case) raise at least five analytic issues:

(1) What are the basic options to be considered in an enforcement decision?
(2) To what *length* should enforcement be pursued? How much is enough?
(3) What difference, if any, does it make whether enforcement is in the hands of public bureaucracies or of private actors (that is, individuals or firms)?
(4) Why is it that enforcement is easier for public bureaucracies to pursue in some circumstances than in others?
(5) Can policies or decisions be made to be 'self-enforcing'? If so, what are the conditions under which that is possible?

Each of these questions will be briefly explored below.

I. BASIC ENFORCEMENT OPTIONS

In each of the eight situations, the 'authorities' (whoever they are) have several possible responses to choose from. Let us consider four:

(1) *Set Aside or Modify the Rule.* They may choose *either* to set aside the rules completely – at least in some cases; *or* to modify the rules in some way, perhaps by bargaining on a case-by-case basis. For example, in case (1), government might decide that it is in a no-win situation with the strikers, and back off or bargain. In case (7), the authorities might concede that Z has a point, and try to work out some alternative arrangements for him which meet the spirit if not the letter of the rules designed to preserve interesting old buildings and to promote safety in domestic appliances.

(2) *Spread the Word.* Rather than abandoning or modifying the rules, the authorities may choose to put the emphasis on publicity and persuasion. For instance, in cases (4) and (5), a campaign might be mounted to tell those involved about the existence of the rules, the reasons for them (the need for conservation of fish stocks to preserve fishermen's livelihoods, the need for funds to pay for the association's activities), how to comply with them, perhaps allied with threats or warnings of the consequences of non-compliance. The store in case (8) might put up posters in sign language indicating that taking goods out of the store without payment is considered to be theft. Such an approach is often termed as a 'compliance' strategy by theorists of enforcement. (See, for instance, Reiss, in Hawkins and Thomas, 1984, pp. 23–35).

(3) *Pursue and Punish Rule Violators.* The emphasis might be put on watching for violations of the rule, pursuing the violators and visiting punishment on them. A variation on the same theme is to reward those who obey – which is in a sense equivalent to 'punishing' those who disobey. For instance, in case (2), the authorities might try to break up the merged company for not observing the conditions under which the merger was permitted. The court in case (8) might clap Y into

gaol. The water authority in case (7) might cut off supply to Z's house. Such an approach is conventially labelled as a 'deterrence' strategy of enforcement.

(4) *Make it Physically Difficult, Impossible or Inconvenient to Break the Rules.* Instead of putting up notices forbidding trespassing (strategy (2)) or watching out for and apprehending trespassers as and when they intrude (strategy (3)), a landowner might discourage trespassers by high walls, thorn hedges, barbed wire. In case (3), the tax might be reconstituted in such a way that it was invisibly deducted, for instance in a multi-stage sales tax, automatically added to the retail price of items that X cannot avoid buying. In case (5), the association might instal gaming machines on its own premises, with an automatic deduction from winnings for the 'house'. In case (8), the store might instal electronic apparatus at the exits, making it impossible to go out with goods that have not been paid for. Technological development offers endless possibilities of this kind of enforcement, just as the advent of typewriters and printers replaced the need to enforce elaborate rules about size and clarity of script and the way that letters are formed (an example given by Perrow (1979, p. 23).

In principle, this array of choices is the same irrespective of whether the enforcement decision is taken by public bureaucracies or by private actors. Is there a single 'correct response' from these options which should always be followed? Should we, for instance, consistently prefer to place the emphasis on the 'softer' enforcement strategies ((1) and (2) above) rather than on the 'harder' strategies ((3) and (4) above)?

The disadvantages of pursuing one set of strategies to the exclusion of the others in *all* conditions are obvious enough. Clearly, always to use strategies (1) and (2) – to bargain or back down in every case, or to bark but never to bite – is to make all rules negotiable and ultimately voluntary. It simply reintroduces the free rider and holdout problem with which this book began. If contracts, agreements, rules or decisions which have been arrived at through some valid procedure are to mean anything, violation must be prevented or punished at least some of the time.

Perhaps less obvious are the disadvantages of always adopting strategies (3) and (4). Isn't that just what is needed for certainty and 'the rule of law'? In the last chapter, we looked at the idea of a 'government of laws and not of men', and to the six conditions explored there should certainly be added mechanistic or automatic enforcement. Indeed, writers such as Lowi (1969) and Thompson (1975) argue eloquently for 'strict rule of law' rather than 'loose administration' and the idea that every decision is bargainable. Lowi (1969, p. 298) wants a return to the 'Schechter rule' once applied by the US Supreme Court, namely that any delegation of power to an administrative agency is invalid if not accompanied by clear standards of implementation.

Let us take this idea to its logical extreme. Consider a community in which there was an 'enforcement machine', in the literal sense. Any violation of any rule would either be impossible or automatically result in punishment. Exactly such a machine figures in a science-fiction story by Sheckley (1974). A person (call him P) is left alone in a camp guarded by a robot. P goes out of the camp for a walk. But, because P has not been told the new password, he cannot get the robot-guard to let him back into the camp when he comes back from his walk. The robot's definitions are very tight and there is no emergency by-pass switch. P has no food, water or shelter, and the climate is such that he will die quickly unless he gets back into the camp. P's companions will not return for some time . . .

That is, of course, the problem with enforcement machines – in real life as well as in science-fiction stories. 'A parking meter will not show understanding or mercy to a person who was one minute over the limit because he was helping a blind man cross the street' (Jowell, 1975, p. 22). A computer-controlled car park in London issued time-stamped tickets to drivers at an entry gate and read the tickets at an exit gate, which automatically opened after payment. Many drivers clenched the tickets between their teeth while looking for a place to park. When they tried to leave the car park, they found themselves trapped at the exit gate, because the machine could not read the soggy tickets . . . Sheckley's story in reverse, in fact. The system had to be scrapped, at great expense. To the extent that any enforcement machine is tamper-proof, it becomes impossible to set aside or modify rules on the spot, in conditions where they are inappropriate or conflicting.

In short, making a fully satisfactory enforcement machine is like aiming for administration by 'rule and rote', as explored in the last chapter. It would require an ability to foresee all possible contingencies, which is rarely – if ever – possible in practice (as in the case of the soggy tickets). Unless that can be done, such a machine may be disastrously inflexible when some extraordinary but compelling reason makes it positively desirable for normal rules to be broken – for example, emergency-service operations which require violations of normal property rights or traffic rules. This harks back to our discussion of rule protases in the last chapter. You may tell your child 'never' to run out of the house into the street, but there are circumstances in which you would certainly want the child to break that rule (fire, explosion). An enforcement machine, for instance which locked the child in the house, would make that impossible. It would also punish or prevent trivial or 'innocent' violations, in which no real harm is done, in just the same way as serious and deliberate ones.

The inflexible enforcement response – sticking 'mindlessly' to the rules, however inappropriate they may be – is traditionally thought of as an occupational disease of hidebound or uncaring petty bureaucrats (Merton, 1949). But the age of automation promises to create just as much, if not more, rule-enforcement inflexibility as the age of 'manual' bureaucracies it is replacing. Most studies of real-life rule enforcement by human agents in fact reveal behaviour which is far from the 'enforcement machine' response. Persuasion, bluff, threats, advice and negotiation tend to figure large (see, for instance, Fenn and Veljanovski, 1983, p. 2). Indeed, Bardach and Kagan (1982) argue that attempts by human enforcement agents to pursue machine-like automatic pursue-and-punish strategies will often tend to destroy the basic aims which rules are designed to secure. They based this conclusion on a study of attempts in the USA during the 1970s to enforce food, housing and workplace safety regulations on the basis of 'objective rules and minimal discretion'.

One of the reasons, then, for avoiding commitment to any one enforcement strategy in *all* cases is the perception that the appropriate response may depend on the type of violation. This kind of analysis is developed by Kagan and Scholz (1984, pp. 67–95), in the context of business regulation. It is summarized in Table 3.1.

Table 3.1: Enforcement responses and types of non-compliance*

		Enforcement response		
		'Soft'		'Hard'
Type of non-compliance	Set aside or modify rule	Inform; guide; counsel; warn	Detect; pursue and punish	Prevent non-compliance by physical structuring
'Unprincipled' 'Incompetent'	Does not diminish incompetence	May change behaviour	May not directly diminish incompetence	Prevents non-compliance *if* feasible and affordable
'Opportunist'	Likely to increase opportunistic evasion	Unlikely to change behaviour	Likely to reduce opportunistic evasion	Prevents non-compliance *if* feasible and affordable
'Principled' (a) Rejection of rule or of specific application	May reduce dissidence without violating basic objectives of rule	Unlikely to change behaviour	May lead to 'martyrdom'	May exacerbate the problem by setting it in concrete
(b) Rejection of authority in general	Admits defeat	Unlikely to change behaviour	May lead to 'martyrdom'	Prevents non-compliance *if* feasible and affordable

**Source:* Adapted from Kagan and Scholz (1984).

'Harder' enforcement strategies ((3) and (4) above) are indispensable where evasion of rules springs from opportunism: that is, where rules will not be obeyed if the chances of evasion going undetected or unpunished (or at least, not heavily punished) are judged to be favourable enough. If a firm adopts a policy of not paying bills until court proceedings are started, the only way to get your money is to do just that. Chester Bowles, head of the US Office of Price Administration during World War II, once said that 20 per cent of the (US) population would automatically comply with any regulation, 5 per cent would attempt to evade it, and the remaining 75 per cent would comply so long as the 5 per cent were caught and punished (Kagan, 1978, p. 75). Economic analyses of punishment invariably focus on opportunistic evasion, assuming that the potential law-breaker weighs up the advantages to him of violating the rules as against the expected cost. Expected cost is the product of the likely penalty if caught and convicted, the probability of detection and the probability of conviction following detection. From that follow deductions about effective levels of deterrence and socially efficient allocation of resources to law enforcement. (The *locus classicus* of this analysis is Bentham's (1931, pp. 325–7) 'rules of punishment'; the approach was resuscitated and converted into modern economic theory by Becker (1968) and Stigler (1970); summaries are given by Posner (1977, pp. 163–78) and Bowles (1982, pp. 72–80).)

Such analyses are interesting and suggestive, since opportunistic evasion can rarely be dismissed in any kind of administration. All the same, not all rule-breaking stems from opportunistic evasion. Quite apart from considerations of cost and effectiveness (to be considered in the next section), the general case against the automatic use of 'harder' enforcement strategies in every case is that, since strict enforcement is necessary only in the absence of consent, it is often better to try to gain consent than to visit sanctions on offenders, and that non-compliance may well be a sign that the decision or rule in question is a bad one and ought to be modified. As we have seen, an 'enforcement machine' approach runs the risk of screening out feedback and exacerbating conflict in ways that might not be necessary.

Indeed, strategy (3) may be unnecessary, inappropriate or even counter-productive as a means of changing behaviour in some cases. For instance, where evasion stems from incompetence or weakness of will rather than from a nice calculation of the probability of detection and punishment, concentrating on penalizing non-compliance is not always the most effective response. Sometimes it may make sense to put resources into helping people to obey (strategy (2)) as well as, or even instead of, punishing them for non-compliance. For instance, punishments will not necessarily modify future behaviour where rules are broken by the confused elderly or by foreigners who do not speak the language of the country (or both, as perhaps applies to case (8)). Sometimes, such a strategy may be appropriate for the population at large, and not just for special groups. Take the case of combating involuntary relapses into left-hand traffic behaviour by Swedish road users after Sweden changed from driving on the left to driving on the right in 1967 (see Silver, 1967; Roalman, 1968; Statens Hogertrafikkommission, 1967, pp. 6–7). In such conditions it is more realistic to see the bulk of the population as willing and eager to comply with the new rule (after all, their lives were at stake in that case), rather than opportunistically weighing up the advantages of non-compliance against the likelihood of detection and punishment. When that is so, it makes sense to 'educate' and 'guide' people struggling to alter long-established reflex habits and skills. Faced with 'incompetent' non-compliance, either of the driving on the right variety or of the confused elderly variety (individuals whose behaviour is not readily modifiable by the threat or use of sanctions), strategies (2) or (4) may be preferable to strategy (3) – that is, counselling, informing or physically preventing non-compliance.

If non-compliance stems from 'principled dissidence' rather than from opportunism or incompetence, the position is different again. Some rules may be broken, not just because the violator thinks that he has an acceptable chance of getting away with it, nor because he is ignorant of, or incapable of obeying, the rule; but rather because he sees it as pointless, unnecessary, ill-conceived, quite inappropriate to his or her particular case or circumstances. Z's action in case (7) may be interpreted as such a response. A classic case of principled non-compliance is the driver who carefully drives through a red traffic light if he believes that the light is stuck on red and the road is clear, even though he knows that red lights mean 'stop' (Kagan, 1978, p. 92).

Applying strategies (3) and (4) to such cases is by no means impossible, but might make things worse rather than better. Motorists might be physically prevented from deliberately driving through red lights by strategy (4), for example by massive steel gates which automatically block the roadway when lights are at red. In Z's case (7), we might imagine a highly sensitive computer-controlled water-supply system capable of sensing any incorrect installation and of immediately shutting off supply. Similarly, non-compliance of such types might be prevented if a sufficiently determined strategy (3) approach was followed by the authorities, if penalties were heavy enough and detection sufficiently vigilant to bring any dissidents into line. The driver might be cowed by such means into either turning round or remaining stationary at the red light for as many hours as it took to summon the authorities and have the lights switched off or repaired. Z might be deterred from all attempts to improve his house, and continue to wash in a bucket. The problem with such responses is that of the 'enforcement machine' more generally. It may not actually be desirable strictly to prevent rule-breaking or to penalize rule-breakers in *all* cases without taking into account the general purpose which the rule is intended to serve and the consequences of obeying the rule in particular instances. The principled dissident may have a good case. Perhaps the rule should be modified. Perhaps some *modus vivendi* can be arrived at through bargaining. Perhaps nothing much will be lost if the rule is simply set aside in circumstances where its strict application might be ridiculous or excessively costly, as in Kelman's example of US workplace safety inspectors demanding that 39 inch guardrails be replaced by 42 inch ones as the regulations require (Kelman, in Hawkins and Thomas, 1984, p. 106). Giving way in one case may not always require giving way in others. Strategy (1) deserves some consideration in such cases, and most real-life rule-enforcement systems have devices for responding in this way. For instance, the US grand jury system, originally imported from England in the seventeenth century, has served through much of its history as a device for introducing political considerations into law enforcement. Grand juries have often set aside the rules for 'principled dissidents' with sufficient local support, even in cases where the formal rules had clearly been broken (Clark, 1975).

On the other hand, where principled dissidence is directed at the general basis of authority on which rules rest, rather than on specific rules or application of those rules, there is nothing much to bargain about. The driver who drives through red lights on principle because he does not recognize the right of the highway authority to interfere with his freedom in any way is rather different from the driver who drives through a light which he believes to be stuck. X's position in case (3) might be interpreted as analogous to the former type of 'dissident', Z's in case (7) as analogous to the latter type (as noted earlier). Strategies (1) and (2) will hardly serve in the former type of case. Strategy (3) may be unavoidable, though, unlike opportunistic evaders, principled dissidents may respond to such an approach by overt last-ditch defiance of authority. Strategy (4) avoids that problem in this kind of case by structuring behaviour physically so that authority in a human form does not enter the scene. This implies shepherding drivers to behave in a certain way by the use of barriers, embankments and road humps rather than by traffic lights, police signals or speed limit signs.

Such an approach, as summarized in Figure 3.1, can thus be applied to a diversity of possible rule-enforcement situations, such as the eight cases given at the outset. It shows that the enforcement decision involves not just the question of *whether* to enforce some rule, policy or agreement, but also the question of *which kind* of approach to enforcement is appropriate to any particular case.

The idea of matching enforcement response to types of non-compliance has some intuitive appeal. A judge, schoolteacher, policeman, anyone in an enforcement role, commonly finds himself modifying the response to violations according to the motives or reasons perceived to lie behind those violations – something that an enforcement machine cannot do. (Many legal penalties, we may note, attach to questions of *intent*, independent of actual results). Tricky and disputable judgements are obviously involved whenever such factors come into consideration. Readers may well differ according to how they interpret the eight cases given at the start, in these terms. Is the 'only took it out to see it in the light' old lady in case (8) incompetent or an opportunist posing as incompetent? Is she really a foreigner or just putting on a foreign accent? Is the firm in case (2) opportunist, incompetent (in that it cannot remember the terms of conditions to which it has agreed) or principled (considers that public authorities have no right to meddle in management decisions or that the requirement to maintain an HQ in A is a patently unworkable one in the current circumstances of the enterprise)?

Moreover, where actual or potential rule-breakers are some mix of opportunists, incompetents and principled dissidents, a real dilemma arises. Picking one general enforcement response on the basis of what is seen to be the commonest type of rule-breaker (for instance, strategy (3) on the basis that opportunism is the main characteristic, as it often is) will not fit all cases of rule violation. On the other hand, trying to modify the response to the circumstances of each case on its merits simply encourages opportunists to masquerade as incompetents or principled dissidents, in order to deflect the 'hard' enforcement response that is really appropriate. Set aside the rule in the case of the motorist who drives through the stuck red light, and you may release a flood of 'I thought the light was stuck' stories from people who want to get home quicker. One crack, and the dam may break, if opportunism is widespread. Again, judgements often differ on the extent to which such an outcome will follow a departure from 'hard' enforcement responses in particular cases. It is the difference of judgement that arises over the categorization of types of non-compliance and over the assessment of the probability of 'soft' enforcement responses offering a crack in the defences which opportunists will turn into a yawning breach, that generates much of the 'politics' of rule enforcement.

II. HOW MUCH IS ENOUGH?

After the basic enforcement response, the next question is *how far* enforcement should be taken, especially when 'harder' enforcement responses (strategies (3) or (4)) are at issue.

Consider four possible criteria which might be applied to this issue. These are summarized in Table 3.2.

Table 3.2: How much enforcement? Four criteria

Level of enforcement activity	Criteria based on *standards* of desired compliance behaviour; costs as an outcome (may be adjusted only by substituting cheaper inputs for more expensive ones)	Criteria based on *costs*, not standards: standards of compliance as an outcome (may be adjusted only by substituting more effective inputs for less effective ones)
Lower	Enforce up to an acceptable level of compliance somewhere between 0 and 100 per cent (criterion (2))	Match marginal enforcement cost against benefits realized from detected cases of non-compliance (criterion (3))
Higher	Enforce up to 100 per cent compliance (criterion (1))	Match marginal enforcement cost against benefits realized from detected cases of non-compliance *plus* benefits of deterring evasion that would occur in the absence of marginal enforcement unit (criterion (4))

(1) Aim for total compliance. It may be that nothing less than 100 per cent compliance will satisfy us in some cases. If that is really so, we must accept whatever costs it takes to achieve that – assuming that it is possible at all. Of course, it may well be that one means of enforcement may be cheaper, for a given level of results achieved, than others. But apart from this, seeking 100 per cent compliance means the pursuit of enforcement without counting the costs. For instance, in case (3), the revenue authorities might raise further court actions and the like to pursue the elusive X to the uttermost farthing, spending whatever was needed to reach that goal. A department store might keep hiring store detectives and/or

installing anti-shoplifting equipment until pilfering completely disappeared.

(2) Aim for an acceptable level of compliance. It may be that some degree of non-compliance is acceptable, so long as it is kept within more or less defined bounds. For instance, in case (1), government may be prepared to ignore lightning or unofficial strikes so long as there is no major official strike. This involves specifying in some rule-of-thumb way a tolerable limit of non-compliance which comes somewhere between 0 and 100 per cent. This may be (as if often the case) extremely vague, consisting of a propensity to crack down when things are perceived to have got out of hand or evasion has become too blatant. As with the 'total compliance' criterion, cost is open-ended, determined by whatever it takes to keep compliance at a tolerable level. Cost can only be contained by substituting cheaper methods for more expensive ones. A department store following this criterion would stop hiring store detectives, etc. when pilfering fell below some stipulated tolerable level – say, 5 per cent of the stock value.

(3) Aim to match (marginal) enforcement cost against benefits directly realized from detecting non-compliance. Criteria (1) and (2) start from desirable or acceptable standards of behaviour. Alternatively, we may start from considerations of *cost*. In a world of scarce resources, enforcement costs may determine acceptable compliance standards, rather than vice versa. It is, for instance, intuitively easier to see the case for a 1 per cent increase in enforcement effort which will raise the compliance level by 60 per cent, than for a 60 per cent increase in enforcement effort which will raise the compliance level by 1 per cent. This is the language of economics. A simple, conventional and down-to-earth economic criterion would be to stop enforcement activity at the point where the cost of adding an extra unit of labour or equipment to the enforcement apparatus is greater than the money value of non-compliance which that extra unit will detect. We stop hiring tax collectors (or bad debts collectors or insurance loss adjusters or welfare fraud inspectors) at the point where the direct cash benefit brought in by the marginal official (in terms of insurance claims disallowed, welfare fraud exposed, unpaid tax recovered) is no more than the cost of employing that official. The department

store stops hiring store detectives at the point where an extra store detective will cost more to hire than the value of the goods which he catches people trying to smuggle out of the store.

(4) Aim to match marginal enforcement cost against benefits directly realized from detecting non-compliance plus benefits of deterring evasion that would occur in the absence of enforcement effort. (3) above is a simple but crude economic criterion. A slightly more sophisticated one, in principle, would count as 'benefits' of the marginal unit of enforcement activity not only the money value of non-compliance which is directly detected *in flagrante* by that unit, but also the money value of non-compliance which would take place in the absence of that unit of enforcement activity but is deterred by it. In other words, we have to consider not only the cash value of claims disallowed by the marginal insurance loss adjuster, but also that of the additional fraudulent claims which *might* have been submitted (by opportunistic evaders whose behaviour is highly sensitive to the number of loss adjusters) in the absence of that official. The department store using this criterion must look, not just at the vaue of goods which the extra store detective intercepts as people try to take them out of the shop, but also the deterrent effect of the extra store detective – i.e. the value of goods that would otherwise be stolen in the absence of that detective.

These criteria are different and at least potentially conflicting with one another. The limits of enforcement are set by target standards of behaviour in criteria (1) and (2) and by cost considerations in criteria (3) and (4). We cannot readily say in advance what the cost of following (1) or (2) might be. Nor can we readily say in advance what might be the overall level of compliance if we follow (3) or (4) – it could be anywhere between 0 and 100 per cent. Criteria (3) and (4) are easiest to follow for user-charge or revenue-producing activities, when benefits can at least in principle be monetized. Criterion (3), although cruder than criterion (4), is easier to put into practice, since the latter tends to involve what philosophers call a counter-factual (that is, the positing of circumstances which do not actually exist). Where benefits cannot readily be monetized on any meaningful scale, criteria (1) or (2) will tend to be used.

In fact, criterion (1) is rarely followed in practice, either by private individuals or by public bureaucracies. First, it may be physically impossible to reach 100 per cent compliance in some cases. Second, all enforcement bureaucracies in practice work within finite budgets, which limit their efforts and force them to be selective in their activities (see Bowles, 1982, p. 73). Third, it is conventionally assumed that prevention and elimination costs rise rapidly as we seek to eliminate non-compliance altogether. We come to deal with progressively more elusive, resourceful and determined rule-breakers, rather than the less dedicated, more visible and more 'amateur'. Costs may also rise as a result of the unwieldiness of the enforcement apparatus itself as it gets larger (for instance, if the enforcers come to number a million people, as in the case of the Soviet KGB, the problem of controlling the controllers becomes a far from trivial one). Sometimes there are effects which run counter to the conventional 'rising marginal cost' assumption. These will be discussed in section V below, when we come to self-enforcement.

Indeed, it is commonly argued that it is normally undesirable to try for 100 per cent compliance with any rule. Such a case is coventionally made on the grounds that it would be wasteful of social resources to do so. The resources allocated to enforcement activity could be put to other, more valued, uses. If we assume:
(a) that the per unit benefits of reducing rule-breaking do *not* rise as we approach 100 per cent compliance:
(b) but that the marginal costs of enforcement rise sharply as we approach that point;
it follows that the cost of enforcement to society is likely to exceed the cost of non-compliance itself at some point. The old maxim *de minimis non curat lex* in part reflects this point. It is admittedly uncomfortable to follow this logic in spheres such as the murder rate or the incidence of rape, although it has to be noted that no society in fact pursues criterion (1) of enforcement even in those fields.

A different way of saying the same thing is to suggest that using criterion (1) can result in enforcement running away with policy. That is, trying to enforce some rule to the point of 100 per cent compliance may have a damaging effect on other important objectives. For instance, it will be little consolation for the department store in our example if the cost of eliminating all pilfering turns out to involve so many store detectives that there is hardly room for customers in the store or to involve such intrusive search and surveillance apparatus that even honest customers decide to shop elsewhere and the store goes bankrupt.

Enforcement can 'run away with policy' in this sense in more than one way. It may involve using methods (such as arbitrary search and seizure) which go against values which may be held to be more important than compliance with the rule in question, (The classic case, of course, is enforcement of Prohibition in the USA from 1920 to 1933: see Simon, Smithburg and Thompson, 1950, p. 21.) Or enforcement may run away with policy in the sense of destroying substantive objectives. For instance, free school meals are provided to British schoolchildren whose parents' income falls below a certain level (in order that they should not be disadvantaged at school on account of hunger), while children from more affluent families have to pay. In December 1977, a campaigning group (the Child Poverty Action Group) highlighted cases of school canteens which had separate tables for 'free meal' and 'paying' pupils, separate queues, and even in one case a separate door into the canteen. Some schools issued different coloured tickets to free-meal children (*Sunday Times*, 1 January 1978). Now there might very well have been genuine 'enforcement' considerations in this kind of treatment (e.g. making sure that nobody got a free lunch who ought to be paying; making sure that free-meal children did not sell their lunch tickets to paying children and spend the proceeds on something else, etc.). But strict enforcement in such cases clearly cuts across the original objective of not disadvantaging poorer children at school.

When levels of rule enforcement are in dispute, the argument typically comes down to a clash between two or more of these four criteria. For instance, 'efficiency' experts often attack bureaucratic enforcement activities on the basis of criterion (3) – i.e. that the cash value of detected non-compliance does not balance the wages of the marginal enforcement official, or even of the average official. Since both of these two items can often be measured without elaborate effort, this is a relatively easy line for an 'outside' critic to pursue. Enforcement bureaucrats can (and often do) counter with arguments based on criterion (4), pointing to the putative cash value of evasion deterred – a factor which, though important to a sophisticated 'marginalist' analysis of the appropriateness of enforcement effort levels, is usually very difficult to measure without laborious and expensive effort, and is thus open to widely differing estimates. Alternatively, the argument may go that one should properly reject the language of cost and benefit altogether. The nature of the case may make it impossible to express costs of benefits of rule compliance in money terms, but the argument turns on what counts as an acceptable level of evasion or whether more enforcement activity is desirable, given that compliance is less than 100 per cent.

Moreover, just as with the array of basic enforcement options considered in the last section, it is common to find that different criteria of enforcement effort levels are argued for in different contexts, even by the same individual or group. Just as we may want to argue for 'softer' enforcement responses in one case but 'harder' responses in another case (e.g. 'hard' enforcement on business violation of safety rules, but 'soft' enforcement on union violation of labour laws, or vice versa), we may argue for cost-determined criteria of enforcement in one case, but for standards-determined criteria of enforcement in another case. Welfare recipients or their spokesmen may attack crackdowns on welfare fraud using criterion (3) – the cash value of money recovered as against the cost of the enforcement effort – as the basis of their argument, but at the same time (or another time) argue for criterion (4) as the basis for tax law enforcement. Taxpayer spokesmen might look at it the other way round. Administrative analysis obviously cannot resolve such political issues. But it should sensitize us to recognize which criterion is in play at any one time, implicitly or explicitly; to be able to identify alternative possible criteria and to be able to identify what information would be needed to establish whether any one criterion is really being followed or not.

III. PUBLIC AND PRIVATE ENFORCEMENT

Up to now, rule enforcement has been discussed in generic terms, posing choices to be faced by whomever the enforcer may be. A third basic choice in enforcement concerns *who* does the enforcing. Is it to be the individual or a public bureaucracy? Where should the balance lie between these alternatives? Consider the following five options:

(1) Put enforcement wholly in the hands of private individuals. Rules of marital fidelity in most societies are enforced in this way. Both the decision over the basic enforcement response (section I above) and the decision on how far to take enforcement (section II) are exclusively made by individuals. Of course, there *could* be a public 'marital fidelity police'. (Why not? Quebec has a public 'language police'.)

(2) Put enforcement mainly in the hands of private individuals. Private actors predominate in enforcing the law of delicts and contracts, in that they do the work of detecting violations, gathering evidence and triggering off the legal process, but some intervention by public bureaucracies may occur as well, for instance in motor traffic accidents.

(3) Divide enforcement between private individuals and public bureaucracies. When it comes to rules against vandalism or theft of property, many aspects of the basic enforcement response decision and the 'how much enforcement' decision are taken by private individuals. This applies especially to the decision on how far to invest in preventive apparatus (option (4) in section I) such as dogs, bolts, bars, locks. But public bureaucracies also partake in such decisions, especially in the matter of how far to take enforcement.

(4) Put enforcement mainly in the hands of public bureaucracies. In the enforcement of statutory regulation of business, public bureaucracies typically predominate. But some degree of private enforcement may take place as well, for instance in the enforcement of the US anti-trust laws. In World War II private citizens voluntarily supplemented the enforcement activities of the US Office of Price Administration by checking prices in retail stores and reporting violations of

the price-control rules to the public authority (Bernstein, 1955, p. 234).

(5) Place enforcement wholly in the hands of public bureaucracies. In fact, absolutely pure cases of exclusively public bureaucracy enforcement are hard to find, since private actors almost always play some part in the detection of violations. But public bureaucracies monopolize much of the process of criminal law enforcement, in that private actors may not in practice bring cases of murder, theft, rape, etc. before the courts in most countries.

Does it make any difference which of these five approaches is taken? Should we be indifferent among them? Not according to many who argue for either more public bureaucracy involvement in law enforcement (for instance, in the sphere of consumer law) or for more private actor enforcement (for instance, voluntary collective action by private individuals in neighbourhood watch schemes to counter theft, vandalism and assault rather than exclusive reliance on a bureaucratized public police force).

In a now well-known article, two famous US economists, Becker and Stigler (1974) looked at two possible ways of improving law enforcement. The first was to raise the rewards of public law-enforcement officials relative to other occupations. Such officials would then suffer heavy costs on dismissal for malfeasance, and the attractions of malfeasance should therefore be reduced. This approach was in fact advocated much earlier by Bentham (1931, p. 396), who observed: 'This excess of salary is like a premium paid for an insurance against [a public bureaucrat's] dishonesty. He has more to lose by becoming a rogue than by remaining honest . . .'

The other, less orthodox, approach was to 'privatize' law enforcement by compensating *anyone* on a performance basis for the enforcement of laws, receiving as compensation the fines levied on convicted violators. As Becker and Stigler put it (1974, p. 19): 'Free competition amongst enforcement firms may seem strange, even terrifying . . . . But society does not pretend to be able to designate who the bakers should be – this is left to personal aptitudes and tastes. Why should enforcers of laws be chosen differently?'

A pure system of private law enforcement in this sense seems to have existed in Iceland between the tenth and thirteenth centuries (Friedman, 1979). In effect, all criminal offences were civil offences, with law-breakers liable to pay a fine to the victim (fines were the principal form of punishment). Even where offences were recognized by the law as 'public' in some sense, the right to pursue the case and to the resulting fine was given to a specific person, if necessary chosen by lot from those affected. All victim claims were marketable, so that they could be sold by the original 'victim' to anyone willing to catch and convict the offender, or to the highest bidder if there were rival enforcement agents competing for the business. Other historical societies, such as the nineteenth-century American West, have put considerable emphasis on private criminal law enforcement, though not to such an extent as this. In eighteenth-century Britain, for instance, the enforcement even of criminal law was largely a private enterprise affair, with little in the way of public police or public prosecution apparatus. For offences punished by fine, the fine was split between the Crown and the law enforcer. For offences punished in other ways, bounties were paid for the apprehension and conviction of offenders (Landes and Posner, 1975; Posner, 1977, p. 462). That, very broadly, is the system to which Becker and Stigler wish to return.

Such proposals sharply direct attention to the question of what difference it makes whether rule enforcement is by public bureaucracies or by private actors. Becker and Stigler claim that where rules are mainly or exclusively enforced by public bureaucracies, the result will be under-enforcement and some degree of corruption (or its diminutives). This, they say, is because the gain to the enforcer under such a system, is often less than the offender's potential penalty. Indeed, as we have already noted, a recurring theme in studies of law enforcement by public bureaucracies is the power of those agents to decide what enforcement response to select, against whom, and how much. Pursuit and punishment (option (3) in section I) is typically used very selectively. The rules are effectively nullified in many cases by the use of option (1). Education, guidance, counselling and warning responses (option (2)) have been observed to be heavily used in spheres such as business regulation and enforcement of court fines (see Bernstein, 1955, p. 223; Cranston, 1979; Bowles, 1982, p. 101; Fenn and Veljanovski, 1983).

Combining 'rigid rules and lax enforcement' (the phrase used by de Tocqueville (1949, p. 75) to describe bureaucratic processes in pre-1789 France) in this way means high potential uncertainty for citizens and considerable discretionary power to public bureaucracies.

What is (or might be) different about a private actor enforcement regime? Becker and Stigler (1974) claim that their scheme of privatized law enforcement would make law enforcement more efficient and transparent. The corruption problem of public law enforcement officials would disappear, since money gains to 'victims' (or those who had purchased victim rights) for enforcement would by definition be the same as punishment costs to violators. Competition among rival law enforcement firms would reduce operational inefficiency (so-called X-inefficiency or organizational slack, of which more in the next chapter), ensuring that enforcement was provided at cost.

Landes and Posner (1975) and Posner (1977, pp. 462–7) argued that Becker and Stigler's proposed system of law enforcement would differ in some rather less desirable ways from a public bureaucracy regime. First, the enforcement level (the choice of criteria (1)–(4) in section II above) would be likely to be different. This is because, in a world of profit-seeking private enforcement firms, enforcement levels would be entirely cost driven rather than standards driven (i.e. criteria (3) and (4) rather than (1) and (2). Moreover, the enforcement level would not be limited by the budgetary check which, as we have seen, operates on public law-enforcement bureaucracies, in consequences of their funding (typically) from more or less fixed annual block budgets. A private enforcement system with access to an efficient private capital market, would not work under a block-budget constraint. It would continue to pursue its enforcement activities as long as those activities were expected to yield a sufficient profit.

Second, where public bureaucracies monopolize or dominate enforcement, they may effectively nullify particular rules by the use of option (1) and section I, laying aside or modifying the rules in particular cases. This is indeed the 'rigid rules and lax enforcement' phenomenon that Becker and Stigler complain about. But a private actor enforcement system might approximate more closely to the 'enforcement machine' considered earlier, with option (1) being used less widely. So long as bounty hunting or fine sharing offered a prospect of sufficient profit, rule-breakers would be pursued, and this might well include trivial cases, or cases of a type which, though clearly violations of the law as written down, do not violate its spirit or are not kinds of behaviour which the framers of the law had in mind to prohibit (such as the ambulance in Gottlieb's 'no vehicles in the park' example mentioned in the last chapter).

Now a public bureaucracy can simply be directed to follow option (1) or (2) where its directorate or political masters fear or dislike the consequences of applying a 'harder' enforcement response to incompetent or 'principled' offenders, or where the rules are otherwise deemed inappropriate. No such mechanism could operate in a private actor enforcement system, except by arbitrary variations in the bounty or fine sharing rules. In so far as a private sector enforcement system would be closer to an 'enforcement machine' than a public bureaucracy system, it would tax the capacity to frame rules with precision to a much greater degree than does a system of enforcement dominated or monopolized by public bureaucracies under political direction. All rules would then have to be framed in such a way as *neither* to leave loopholes (unintentionally allowing activities which we really want to forbid) *nor* to go to the opposite pole and unintentionally forbid activities which we really want to allow. Now, as we noted in the last chapter (section IX), the easy way for rule-makers to deal with the loophole problem is to write the rules over-inclusively, forbidding behaviour which it is not really intended to punish, and leaving it to enforcers to apply the rules sensibly. This easy option could not be used in a private actor enforcement system without producing bizarre effects arising from zealous pursuit of bounties or fine shares.

Third, the overall enforcement level would be conditioned by the design of the bounty or fine-sharing structure, at least for criminal law. This presents real design difficulties. It has already been mentioned that the standard Benthamite analysis of criminal punishment seeks to fix an expected penalty for rule-breaking (the product of probability of conviction and the size of the likely penalty if convicted) which will normally deter the opportunist who is thinking of breaking a rule. Where the probability of conviction is 1 (conviction is certain, in other words), the penalty should exceed the costs to the victim (if there is one) of rule violation. This is in order to encourage people where possible to engage in voluntary transactions rather than forced exchanges (the essence of most criminal offences), with law courts clumsily determining the terms of the 'transaction' *ex post facto*.

But the penalty should equally not be set so far above the costs to the victim that a calculating person will *never* break the rule, in conditions where the private benefits of doing so exceed the social cost. Suppose that someone is injured or about to give birth. She is in a deserted place. She needs to get to a hospital quickly. She comes across an unattended vehicle. She steals it to get to the hospital. Had she been able to treat with the owner, she would have offered more for the use of the vehicle than its temporary loss would have cost the owner. Almost certainly, the latter would have been ready to do a deal. To set penalties too high above victim costs is 'socially inefficient', in that it prevents resources from moving from less to more valued uses.

Having fixed the desirable level of punishment for the circumstance where conviction is certain, the next step in the standard analysis is to save on the resources employed in enforcement activities and adjust the penalty scales accordingly. If the desirable level of cost imposed by punishment on the offender is set at 100 where conviction is certain, the same expected cost can be achieved by raising the penalties and decreasing the likelihood of detection and conviction by devoting fewer resources to enforcement. If we cut down on the enforcement effort so that the probability of conviction drops from 1 to 0.1 (only 1 chance in 10 of being convicted, on the average), we must raise the penalty to 1000 to achieve the same expected cost of 100 ($1000 \times 0.1 = 100 \times 1$). Indeed, in order to save enforcement costs, the absolutely 'ideal' schedule of penalties is one in which the cost imposed by punishment on detected and convicted offenders approaches infinity and the probability of detection approaches zero (Posner, 1977, pp. 163–8).

To the extent that this logic is followed in devising punishment codes (the practical difficulties of doing so are obvious enough), it would be difficult in principle to send the right signals to criminal law enforcers in a private actor law enforcement system financed by bounties and fine-sharing. Under a fine-sharing system, offences punished by heavy penalties which were intended to *save* on social resources devoted to law enforcement, would send exactly the opposite signal to the enforcers. The latter would have incentives to concentrate more efforts on high fine offences, not less. This would be likely to raise the probability of conviction, so that the level of overall resources devoted to law enforcement was greater than was necessary or desirable, in terms of the orthodox analysis sketched out earlier. Such an outcome could only be prevented by fixing the bounties or shares of fine payable to enforcers at a low level relative to the penalties meted out by the courts to convicted offenders. Becker and Stigler (1974, p. 16) themselves proposed to deal with the problem by an 'appropriate tax on private enforcement'. But that would obviously be a certain recipe for bribery and corruption as private law enforcers entered into collusive deals with detected violators, to keep the latter out of court. The prospect of having to conclude such deals, it is true, might very well have a deterrent effect on potential violators analogous to the effect of court fines. But there would still be likely to be over-enforcement in the sense of 'too much' law enforcement activity and 'too high' expected punishment costs.

This kind of argument is fairly abstract and Becker and Stigler's proposal is, of course, an extreme one. But it does serve to draw attention to alternative ways of institutionalizing law enforcement. Such enforcement is seldom completely monopolized in all its aspects by public bureaucracies; and the balance does *in fact* shift among approaches (1), (2), (3), (4) and (5) over time and space, in fields such as bankruptcy law, consumer law, competition law – even, as we have seen, criminal law.

Moreover, this debate serves to show that there *are* some reasons for expecting a different consequence according to which mix of public bureaucracy and private actor enforcement is chosen, in terms of the ways that the enforcement option and level of enforcement decisions are approached. A public bureaucracy-dominant system (i.e. options (4) and (5) in this section) generates a potential 'rigid rules and lax enforcement' problem. A private actor-dominant system (options (1) and (2)) has no such inherent bias. But in so far as the latter may tend to approximate more closely to an 'enforcement machine', it may demand a degree of precision in framing effective rules and efficient penalties which is in practice infeasible.

IV. EASE OF ENFORCEABILITY IN BUREAUCRATIC ENFORCEMENT

A fourth major issue in enforcement concerns the extent to which design or foresight can enhance the 'enforceability' of rules. It is a common observation that some rules are easier to enforce than others. What are the factors which tend to make enforcement easier or more difficult?

This section explores the factors affecting ease of enforceability in conditions where rules are mainly enforced by public bureaucracies and where the relevant population contains a sizeable number of opportunists who will break the rules if they expect to benefit by so doing. The next section looks at the possibility of 'self-enforcement' more generally.

Let us take an hypothetical case which shows how to do enforcement the hard way. Suppose that an annual tax is levied on domestic pets at a rate proportionate to their value. Suppose the case for such a tax to be that times are hard, pets are a luxury and that the more exotic, and therefore expensive, is the animal kept as a pet, the more of a luxury it is. But we may fairly confidently predict that, given opportunism, such a tax would present major enforcement difficulties for a tax bureaucracy in most circumstances.

Such a tax would be likely to be a nightmare to enforce for five reasons:

(1) The relevant population is hard to identify. We may assume that there is no central register covering all types of pets

and their owners. The tax bureaucracy would have to start from scratch in assembling that information, and indeed it would be almost impossible to maintain such a register accurately. Many animals kept as pets have a fairly short life-span, are capable of reproducing rapidly, may be casually exchanged among children, may be killed at any time by predators. Moreover, there are likely to be rule category problems, such as were discussed in the last chapter. Many pets are difficult at the margin to distinguish from wild animals, farm animals or working animals. (Is a guard dog a 'pet'? If not, how might pet dogs be distinguished from guard dogs? What if a dog is kept partly as a pet and partly as a guard dog?) Given that opportunists could exploit all of these factors, the verification of details of the pet register would be, to put it mildly, a laborious process.

(2) There is no convenient point at which to impose a control regime. We may assume that there is no monopoly supplier or small group of suppliers of all kinds of pets who can be harnessed as tax collectors. The number of pets supplied through commercial establishments or breeding societies may be quite small as a proportion of the total, especially for pets such as cats or rodents. One is faced with a mass of individual owners, many of whom (we may suppose) are minor children, who cannot be directly held liable for tax except through their parents or guardians. The latter in turn may be honestly – or opportunistically – unaware of everything that their charges do. Children may deceive their parents; may keep pets other than at home; may keep them jointly with other children so that no single individual can easily be identified as the person who ought to be liable for tax. If such problems were avoided by exempting, say, 'children's pets' from tax, adult opportunists would naturally seek wherever possible to shift nominal ownership of pets to minor children.

(3) The unit of value (the basis of the tax) is inherently hard to fix. Many pets are obtained and disposed of outside the market economy altogether. There is no equivalent to the record of stock market transactions which acts as a central, convenient and authoritative source of ascertaining the value of listed stocks at any point in time. To do the valuation job properly, each pet would have to be assessed separately each

year, taking into account factors such as age, deformities, injuries, physical beauty, fertility, etc. That opinions might differ on the assessment of such matters is rather more than a theoretical possibility.

(4) As it stands, the tax would be hard to reinforce by checks from other enforcement 'sites'. It might perhaps be possible to imagine a few areas where reinforcing checks might be built in. For example, customs clearance on animals being imported, the system for releasing pets from quarantine, the regulation of commercial dog and cat kennels, the arrangements for rounding up stray dogs and cats, might be some of the points where checks could be made to reinforce the administration of the pet tax. But it is difficult to imagine such reinforcement playing a large part in this scheme. Essentially, the pet tax bureaucracy would be on its own.

(5) Incentives for compliance are weak. This is a development of point (4) above. Not only is there an absence of different vantage-points from which the enforcement of the tax might emanate. There is also nothing to be gained or lost in people's other dealings with public bureaucracies by paying or failing to pay the pet tax. Paying the pet tax is not a precondition for enjoying other kinds of benefits, or avoiding other penalties. For example, the pet tax cannot (we shall suppose) be offset to any degree against other taxes. Pets on which tax has not been paid are, in the main, not likely to command a substantially lower market price than tax-paid ones. The payment of tax is not linked up in a package deal with offsetting benefits, such as free veterinary checks at the tax office.

The pet tax is, of course, a fiction. But by working back from the likely difficulties which it would run into, we can see some of the factors which govern ease or difficulty of enforcement tasks by public bureaucracies. These factors can be more generally – but perhaps rather ponderously – termed (a) cadasterability or listability, (b) conduitability or capacity for canalization, (c) standard unequivocality (d) reinforceability or redundancy, and (e) 'cross-sanctions'. Taking these in turn:

(a) *Cadasterability* or *listability* means that the population to which a scheme applies is readily identifiable without minute and case-specific research, if possible from sources which are available in advance. It also means that the enforcee population is relatively stable, since it will obviously be harder to achieve where that population is highly volatile or for enterprises that lack continuous operation. For instance, if the pet tax were to be limited to pedigree animals – which are by definition listed in a central register for each breed – it would instantly become much more cadasterable. A tax on holders of registered securities would be more cadasterable than a tax on holders of bearer bonds.

(b) *Conduitability* or capacity for *canalization* means that the blameable units are stable, clearly defined, specific rather than diffuse, and above all, relatively few in number, so that the enforcing bureaucracy can operate through a relatively small number of channels or bottlenecks at which oversight can be economically applied. A tax on commercial sale of pet foods, for instance, would be much more conduitable than a tax on pet owners in general. Attempts to canalize operations are a recognizable stage in the history of most bureaucratic enforcement schemes, and non-conduitability is a rock on which such schemes commonly founder.

For instance, it is easier to enforce maximum production quotas on milk than on cereals in the UK because the former is highly conduitable, whereas the latter is not. Virtually all the milk produced in the UK is bought by government marketing boards, so that the output of each producer is fairly easy to monitor. But this does not apply to cereals, for which there is no equivalent to the milk marketing boards. Cereal can easily be sold by producers to neighbours, fed to pigs, etc., without passing through any concentrated marketing apparatus. Similarly, conduitability problems in the form of ambiguous blameability haunt many kinds of business regulation: Is the corporation liable for violations as a legal person, or are its officers or directors? (Stone, 1975). Exactly the same difficulty applies to labour unions, especially where (as in the UK) decision-making formally takes place by votes of the mass membership. That can make it hard to fix what is the unit blameable for illegal behaviour by union members. Attempts to conduit liability by fixing on the leadership or corporate legal personality as the blameable unit may simply lead to unofficial strikes or picketing behaviour strategically disowned by the union leadership, in which case enforcement activity can hardly avoid turning to individuals as the blameable units. This is, of course, decidedly awkward where there are a great many of them, as in the example of case (1) given at the outset of this chapter.

Quite apart from the 'canalizability' dimension of conduitability, the stability dimension is often the source of enforcement problems. This is the familiar 'fly-by-night' problem, where the transience of blameable units defeats efforts at rule enforcement. Examples are the fraudulent travel agent who obtains a large number of blank air tickets from airlines, sells them to customers and then goes into liquidation so that the airlines cannot recover their money; or the construction enterprise which incorporates a company for each development project and winds it up at the end of the project so that dissatisfied purchasers, etc. are left with no one to sue.

(c) *Standard unequivocality* harks back to the discussion of rule protases in the last chapter. It means that enforcement rests on standards or values which can be ascertained relatively economically as well as 'objectively'. The pet tax raises impossible difficulties in this respect. Its basis of value is case-specific and infinitely arguable. Substituting values based on objectively and economically ascertainable characteristics – such as type of animal, size, weight, number of legs – would make the tax much more standard-unequivocal. Where enforcement rests on extensive hypothetical or counter-factual judgements (for example, valuing goods which are not for sale or on a basis which assumes them to be somehow other than they are) is almost bound to be costly and difficult, potentially lending itself to endless disagreement, differences of interpretation, calls for arbitration and appeals.

(d) *Reinforceability* means cross-checking oversight from different vantage-points, established for different purposes. For instance, checks on the tax liability of a dead person's estate typically reinforce checks on tax paid during life. Checks on persons leaving a country may be used as a means of enforcing tax payment. Sales tax checks may be used to reinforce checks on payment of annual licence taxes for items such as guns, TV sets, cars. Bentham's (1931, pp. 415–16) example of this was the way in which the once notorious delay in the delivery of mails in Britain was halved by combining the mail-delivery service with the carriage of passengers between town, so that the postmen became subject to pressures for celerity from their passengers as well as from users of the mail service.

In some ways, this is a special case of 'conduitability', since it involves the exploitation of convenient sites for economical enforcement of several rules at once. Indeed, often the neatest and most economical way of establishing a bureaucratic enforcement apparatus is to avoid new special purpose creations altogether, but simply to latch on to existing control sites established for other reasons, with a minimum of adjustment or modification. (We shall come back to this in Chapter 5.)

(e) *'Cross-sanctions'* means that those who contemplate breaking a rule are put in a position where they must offset the advantages of violating one rule against corresponding disadvantages which automatically come into play. It is closely related to reinforceability, but goes beyond it by enmeshing the would-be rule-breaker in a system of countervailing incentives such that violation of one rule causes other rules to work to the violator's disadvantage. For example, evasion of the rule requiring registration of births, deaths and marriages may automatically cut off entitlement to benefit payments or tax reliefs. Failure to pay stamp taxes on documents may mean that those documents cannot be taken as evidence in a law court. Failure to file tax returns or company reports may cut off eligibility for government contracts or licences. Under-declaring income to minimize tax liability may automatically cut borrowing ability and the value of tax offsets. The British Purchase Tax introduced in 1940 was originally built on a 'cross-sanctions' principle, since all goods on which tax was not paid were subject to price control, and all goods not subject to price control were liable to tax (Hood, 1985). The term 'cross-sanctions' comes from Bernstein (1955, pp. 245–5), building on the work of Landis (1938, p. 244).

The importance of these enforceability factors extends well beyond taxation. They can rarely be excluded from consideration in any scheme where opportunism combines with bureaucratic enforcement. Awareness of such factors may help us both to spot enforceability 'niches' as they open up and also to notice when and why the going for bureaucratic enforcement gets harder. As will be shown in Chapter 5, social and economic change both creates and destroys administrative properties such as cadasterability, conduitability and standard-unequivocality.

Moreover, explicating such factors can help us to understand the potential conflicts in policy design when enforcement is at issue. The five enforcement factors itemized above often conflict with one another in reality. For instance, consider two alternative rules to cope with a high incidence of traffic accidents between pedestrians and poorly maintained buses: (a) all bus operators must maintain their vehicles' brakes to a standard of not less than 85 per cent efficiency; (b) all pedestrians must wear special crash helmets and protective clothing. Both rules score fairly high on cadasterability. Rule (a) scores high on conduitability (there might be a problem with 'fly-by-night' bus operators, of course), but rather less high on standard unequivocality, reinforceability and cross-sanctions. Rule (b), on the other hand, scores low on conduitability but high on standard-unequivocality, since anyone could tell at a glance whether a pedestrian is wearing a crash helmet or not, whereas finding out whether the brakes of a bus are operating to more or less than 85 per cent efficiency requires special equipment and research. Short of settling for both rules, in a belt-and-braces solution to the problem, some trade-off of these different enforceability profiles would be required.

An understanding of such enforceability factors also helps us to recognize potential conflicts in policy design between considerations of enforceability in general and other criteria. For example, 'cadasterability' may run up against ideas for directing operations to a population which cuts across any existing registration category. Conduitability may run up against ideas about minimum restrictions on behaviour. Unequivocal standards may be regarded as undesirably crude, lumping together items that ought to be separated. Principles of reinforceability and 'cross-sanctions' may be seen as unfair or even illegal (as in business regulation in the USA). As we saw earlier, enforcement can sometimes run away with policy, and we may well want to avoid that. If ease of enforceability were all that was wanted, the five enforceability factors reviewed here could serve as basic design criteria. The problem, of course, is that usually enforcement if *not* all that is wanted.

V. SELF-ENFORCEMENT?

To what extent can rules be enforced without the heavy hand of public bureaucracy? 'Self-policing' and 'self-enforcement' are terms in common currency, but often used vaguely. Perhaps there are four possible senses of 'self-enforcement', two of which we have already encountered. These are:

(1) Enforcement physically built in to a structure. We have already looked at rule enforcement by built-in physical or mechanical processes – that is, option (4) considered in section I. This can be counted as 'self-enforcement' in that it avoids or reduces the need for bureaucratic enforcement, for instance in the design of street layouts that deter mugging, vehicle theft, even riots. As we saw, technological development promises to add to the possibilities of such self-enforcement, but it has built-in limitations too. That is, physical self-enforcement is not always feasible. It is often very expensive to set up and operate. It is less inherently flexible than enforcement based on rules which can be broken.

(2) Communal solidarity. Since enforcement is needed only if there is conflict or dissent, a high degree of social solidarity may make bureaucratic policing unnecessary. Rule enforcement is then built into the social fabric, provided automatically or spontaneously rather than artificially by some special force. A community might be so public-spirited (or so socially conditioned) that either no rules are ever broken or that any non-compliance is readily detected and dealt with by the citizenry at large. It seems, for example, that in the 400 years that the island of St Kilda was inhabited as a civilian settlement, no crime was ever recorded and no policeman ever called for (Steel, 1975, p. 33). Needless to say, this degree of solidarity typically does not exist in large-scale and complex settlements, and even in small simple communities it has its decidedly negative side (the lynch mob, the witch hunt). But it

always can be more or less, and the greater the extent to which it exists, the less is the need for bureaucratic enforcement.

(3) Private enforcement by victims or agents. Even without communal solidarity, self-enforcement in another sense is possible. First, as has already been shown, there are many spheres in which the bulk of law enforcement is in the hands of private individuals, not public bureaucracies. This tends to apply where there is a clear victim who stands to suffer from a violation – unlike, say, bribery, prostitution, gambling, tax evasion, where the 'victims' are very diffuse (see Posner, 1977, pp. 171, 468–9). Where the victim is likely to know the identity of the violator and where it is hard to conceal the offence (as in contract law), private enforcement tends to prevail. Some, as we saw in section III, would like to apply that principle to other kinds of law enforcement as a substitute for discretionary enforcement by public bureaucracies.

Second, even where bureaucratic enforcement formally prevails, some private enforcement is typically incorporated into the enforcement structure. This may be done, for instance, by granting privileges which their possessors must then act to enforce. If I get an exclusive franchise to sell ice-cream on the beach, it will be in my interest to tell the relevant authorities about any unlicensed rivals who appear on the beach, even if I do not physically remove 'pirate' vendors myself. The same result can be achieved if enforcement is tightly imposed on some sub-group of the total population which is highly vulnerable to enforcement activity because of conditions such as cadasterability or conduitability (for instance, owners of pedigree animals, in the pet tax case). Those who are inescapably caught in the net then have an incentive spontaneously to inform on rule-breaking by 'pirates' or 'cowboys' who are less vulnerable to enforcement (for instance, small marginal enterprises as against large well-established ones). Tax and regulatory schemes typically rely heavily on self-enforcement in this sense to supplement bureaucratic enforcement.

(4) Enforcement through membership institutions. Self-enforcement can be taken further than this when standard setting and punishment, as well as detection of non-compliance, is carried out other than through public

bureaucracies. As mentioned above, that may occur if the citizenry in general is unusually harmonious and public-spirited. But in modern societies the typical form is that of enforcement through specialized membership associations rather than conventional public bureaucracy.

This involves buttressing or blessing institutions which discipline their own members in respect of a code of conduct devised and interpreted by itself. This carries conduitability, cadasterability and standard-unequivocality to its logical conclusion. That is, all the work of enforcement is done by some 'conduit' authority. Those to whom the rules apply are the members of that authority (cadasterability). The rules are interpreted and devised by representatives of the group to which they apply (as a way of dealing with the standard-unequivocality problem which arises under bureaucratic enforcement).

Self-enforcement of this kind is widely applied to specialized areas of activity dominated by powerful groups or associations – such as legal or medical conduct, or fair trading rules in financial markets. In the extreme case, public power is conveyed to the membership association, for instance in giving it the legal right to discipline members for misconduct. (A well-known example is Lloyd's of London, an insurance under-writing association. Its members are exempt from the law governing UK insurance companies but its Council is required by law to operate a self-regulatory regime and is empowered to issue legally binding directives to members for that purpose.) Alternatively, self-enforcement by a membership association may spring from fears or threats of regulation by public bureaucracy if too many scandals break out, rather than by putting public power in the hands of the association.

Self-enforcement by membership associations means that rules can be adapted, interpreted and applied by those close to the action, and it can mean that the spirit as well as (or even instead of) the letter of the rules is enforced. It is capable of rapid adaptation and it is cheap, at least in the superficial sense that it saves on the costs of public bureaucracy. But such self-enforcement certainly has its limits. First, the main sanction on which enforcement rests (expulsion or suspension of membership), though powerful, is typically too clumsy to use as a means of disciplining any but the grossest violations of good conduct rules. Second, such associations can only be expected to enforce regulations which are broadly in line with the interests of the group in general. A group or profession may, of course, take an 'enlightened' view of its social responsibilities. But they will naturally stop short of measures which will seriously harm the interests of the members as a group. Third, such associations cannot be conjured up out of nothing, and if they are, they are likely to be discredited or ignored. An industry with intensive competition among a multitude of small firms, or a community sharply divided into two or three rival groups, will be less fertile ground for such self-enforcement than a cartelized industry or a community dominated by a single powerful group or association.

VI. SUMMARY AND CONCLUSION

Enforceability is, or ought to be, central to administrative analysis. Decisions, laws, court judgements, do not enforce themselves. History is a graveyard of rules which may (or may not) have been a good idea in principle, but proved impossible to enforce – laws forbidding gambling, smoking, drinking, football, the keeping of dogs. MacDonagh's (1961, p. 205) description of the rules made to govern emigrant ships leaving Britain for America in the nineteenth century as 'a paper regimentation with as little relation to the world of facts as the decrees of the Emperor Seth', could apply just as well to rules in many other times and places.

This chapter has:

(1) Explored the choices involved in rule enforcement, in relation to *how* to enforce, *how much* to enforce and *by whom* to enforce. It is rare to find that there are no alternatives in these matters or that there is one single, all-purpose, best approach to enforcement. In principle, the options can be reviewed systematically. These choices are to some degree related to one another since, as we have seen, the choice of the public bureaucracy private actor mix in enforcement may have an impact on enforcement response and level. Profit-seeking private enforcers are less likely to choose 'softer' (compliance)

enforcement options than public bureaucracies, especially where the latter dominate the enforcement process. They are also likely to follow different criteria relating to enforcement level, namely criteria (1) and (3) in section II rather than (2) or (4). The latter criteria are more likely to be the watchword of public bureaucracies.

(2) Explored the factors which determine the ease or difficulty of rule enforcement by public bureaucracies, and what is involved in arrangements that might be described as self-enforcement in some sense – i.e. enforcement other than by public bureaucracies alone. This can serve to identify the factors which helped or hindered enforcement in a study of cases after the event. It may help to explain why some efforts to enforce rules fail, are likely to fail, or come to fail having once succeeded. But it may also help to improve awareness of the enforceability factor at the design stage. Some of these factors, to be sure, are immanent rather than readily designable. But a designer must be able to work with nature and to know what immanent factors to look for.

QUESTIONS FOR REVIEW

1. Is a detect-and-punish approach always the best way to tackle rule violation?

2. Should enforcement efforts aim to reduce rule violation to zero?

3. At the time of writing, the Thai government is planning to enforce health and environmental laws by using unemployed university graduates as enforcement agents. The reward of those agents is to come from 50 per cent of any fines collected as a result of information supplied. How would you expect the results of this enforcement scheme to differ from enforcement by bureaucrats on fixed salaries, and (given opportunism) what problem would you foresee?

4. Suppose that accident and pollution risks in a popular sea-bathing area lead the authorities (a) to forbid

underwater tricycle racing by scuba-divers, for safety reasons, (b) to forbid dogs and cats from swimming in the sea, for public health reasons (the latter was actually done by the Greek government in 1983). What difficulties of enforcement would you expect these measures to encounter? What alternative approaches might be tried?

5. Suppose that government decides to tax diamonds. It is considering: (a) an annual tax on owners of diamonds according to the value of the gems they own: (b) a tax on insurance premiums for diamonds, payment of such tax to be a precondition of a valid insurance contract. Which option do you think would be easier to enforce, and why?

GUIDE TO FURTHER READING

Posner (1977, pp. 163–78, 461–78) and Bowles (1982, pp. 50–105) give clear accounts of economic analysis of law enforcement. Bernstein (1955, pp. 217–49) contains many insights into the enforcement problem faced by US regulatory bureaucracies, but the factual detail and analytic approach is out of date. Kagan, on his own (1978) and with others (Bardach and Kagan, 1982; Kagan and Scholz, in Hawkins and Thomas, 1984, pp. 67–95) has developed an interesting analysis of the limitations of the strict 'penal' approach to rule enforcement, which has been much drawn upon here.

4 Providing Services: Organization

'In one massive building in Washington some government employees
are working full-time to devise and implement plans to spend our
money to discourage us from smoking cigarettes. In another massive
building ... other employees are working full-time spending our
money to subsidize farms to grow tobacco ...' (Friedman and
Friedman, 1980, pp. 291-2)

The design and enforcement of rules is basic to any kind of
administration. As we have seen, some public good (or bad)
problems can be tackled by no more than the framing and
enforcement of a compulsory membership rule to foreclose
holdouts. For instance, if failure to clean the common parts of
an apartment building may cause discomfort and disease, it
may suffice to deal with the problem merely by a rule requiring
each tenant to share in cleaning, and prescribing suitable
penalties for non-participation.

Such a rule, of course, only stops opting out. It leaves all the
details to be worked out as to how the cleaning job is actually to
be done. But public services are not brought by storks. Their
provision has to be organized by assembling resources and
applying them to concrete tasks. It goes without saying that
such organization is often problematic. News media feed us a
stream of stories about the failings of public service provision –
delay, poor service, contradictory or misleading information,
inefficiency and confusion, the left hand destroying what the
right has built up. The staple service inefficiency stories come
up again and again – the letter that takes six weeks to be
delivered across three blocks; the driver's licence issued in error
to a dog or a blind person; the broom handles or drain covers
bought for public services at absurdly high prices or in
ridiculously large quantities; the aid supplies to disaster areas

which arrive late or at the wrong time or place and contain items either grotesquely inappropriate for the problem in hand or in such poor condition that they have to be laboriously thrown away . . . and so on. Nor are these peculiarly twentieth-century problems. For instance, the famous eighteenth-century radical, Jeremy Bentham, began a lifetime's study of public organization as a result of naively asking why it had to be that charges should be so exorbitant and service so poor in the legal bureaucracy of his day (Bentham, 1931, p. ix).

This chapter looks at the range of basic choices to be made in organizing the production of public services. One such choice – the distinction between public bureaucracy and private or independent enterprise – was discussed in the last chapter, in the context of law enforcement. That issue will be revisited below in relation to public services more generally. But simply opting for private enterprise or public bureaucracy provision by no means exhausts the basic design choices involved in organizing public services, as the following sections try to show.

I. BASIC ISSUES IN ORGANIZATION

Let us start with the basics. Consider the apartment block cleaning problem which was mentioned earlier. Having dealt with holdouts by compelling everyone to pay or to participate, what are the options open to the tenants in actually getting the cleaning job done? Initially, four alternatives might be considered:

(1) Each tenant might be made responsible for doing some allotted part of the job in person. Some further rules would then be needed to avoid overlaps and underlaps, in that some rota would have to be fixed and/or demarcation lines agreed between one tenant's area of responsibility and another's.

(2) Some or all tenants might individually contract with others to carry out their obligations in their stead (just as people subject to military service obligations in the past were often able to send substitutes rather than to serve in person). This is a small but significant modification of (1).

(3) The tenants might as a group make a deal with a person

or enterprise to clean the whole building. In that case, the demarcation of work problem (as in (1) and (2) above) would not arise, but the period of the contract and the performance required of the contractor would have to be specified, and there would have to be rules covering how costs would be shared among tenants and how the tenants should collectively decide on the terms of a proposed cleaning contract.

(4) Instead of (3), the tenants as a group might directly employ cleaners on a master–servant basis – i.e. with an open-ended contract period and an obligation on the employee to work as directed rather than with performance standards specified in advance. In that case, rules would be needed to fix who would supervise the employee and what that employee would do if (as is quite likely) he or she were given contradictory instructions by different tenants. The tenants would also have to agree some procedures for hiring and firing, for handling pay reviews or responding to pay-rise demands, and so on.

Options (1)–(4) are alternative ways that the tenants might collectively choose to do the job if the rule requiring cleaning did not go beyond compulsory membership or payment to specify how the job of cleaning was actually to be done. Of course, it is quite possible to frame a rule which completely foreclosed the choice of alternative ways of going about the task, by laying down exactly how the task was to be carried out. Indeed, once one moves from simply preventing non-participation to specifying precisely how the service is to be performed, other possibilities can be added to options (1)–(4) above. For instance:

(5) The tenants might be obliged to pay compulsory levies to some *stipulated* enterprise charged with the task of cleaning apartment buildings. Within such a general arrangement, of course, many variants might be possible. For instance, would there be a single monopoly supplier (as with automobile roadworthiness tests in Germany or Sweden) or might users be able to choose from an 'approved list' of designated enterprises (as with automobile testing in the UK)? Would the service providing enterprises be public bureaucracies, private companies, membership associations?

(6) Performance of the service and payment might be

completely separated, in that the cleaning work might be done by designated enterprises which were financed annually out of a general tax fund rather than from specific levies on the tenants as such. A parallel might be drawn with the arrangements for cleaning the public roadways in most places.

This indicates only in the sketchiest possible way some of the options for organizing a very simple public service. But it throws up six key dimensions of the public service organization problem which will be discussed in the sections that follow. These are:

> *Specialization* (i.e. do all tenants function as part-time do-it-yourself cleaners, or do they use a specialist for the job?).
> *Scale of organization* (i.e. is the cleaning service to be organized for each apartment block separately, or for apartment blocks in general?).
> *Employment* versus *specific contract arrangements* (i.e. do the tenants hire a cleaner, or make a deal with a contract-cleaning enterprise?).
> *Single authorized provider* (private or public) versus *some rivalry among potential providers.*
> *User-charge or earmarked tax-based provision* versus *provision financed from general taxation.*
> *Public bureaucracy* versus *private provision* (as in the law-enforcement case in the last chapter).

Other dimensions could of course be added. But these must serve for the discussion of this chapter. Each of these choices will be briefly discussed in the sections which follow.

II. DO-IT-YOURSELF PUBLIC SERVICES OR USE OF SPECIALISTS?

We saw in the apartment cleaning example that one way of providing a public service is to make the people concerned do the job themselves. Compulsory part-time military service is perhaps the prime example, and the same principle has been applied on occasion to road repairs, street lighting, snow clearing and many other public services. There are many possible variants on the theme. In the apartment cleaning case, each tenant might be obliged to clean a particular section outside his flat every week; there might be a rota by which each tenant in turn was responsible for cleaning the common parts as a whole; the tenants might draw lots each week for the job (the public auditors of ancient Athens were chosen periodically by lot). Even when participation is not compulsory, public services may be provided in part or whole by part-time volunteers, on an unpaid or token-payment basis. The term 'co-production' is sometimes used to refer to cases where consumers help to produce the services they use (see Ostrom and Ostrom, in Savas, 1978, pp. 33–5).

Such an arrangement has some potential advantages. Since the consumers and producers of the service are the same people, it may help to prevent the conflicts that might otherwise arise between producers and consumers, masters and employees, customers and contractors (over pay, charges, skimping of service, shirking on the job) and which often figure large in dissatisfaction with public services provided by specialists (be they public bureaucracies or contractors). 'Rip-off artistry', vested interest in perpetuating a particular type of service for which the need is past, insensitivity to new demands, should be minimized in this kind of arrangement.

'New left' writers like Illich in the 1970s made fashionable the idea of doing-it-yourself rather than relying on specialized providers in matters such as education and health care (see Illich, 1972). Ten years later, Naisbitt (1982, pp. 131–57) claimed that there was a general trend in the USA away from reliance on specialized institutions for particular services towards 'self-help' or do-it-yourself involvement in service provision. His examples included neighbourhood watch groups in crime prevention; the hospice movement for the terminally ill; a massive increase in the number of children being educated at home, as a reflection of loss of confidence in schools; even survivalist groups seeking to protect themselves from the effects of nuclear war rather than relying on others to do so. Many innovative public services are organized in the form of self-help ventures and network groups.

The main problem with non-specialist organization, especially when service is compulsory, is conventionally argued to be its potential inefficiency in what is called an 'allocative' sense. That is, waste arises when allocative rules stop resources from moving from less valued to more valued uses. A rule obliging all tenants to take part in person in cleaning the common parts of their apartment building could lead to this kind of inefficiency. If strictly enforced, it would stop tenant A, who has no taste or aptitude for cleaning, but who can use his talents more productively in other ways, from offering to pay tenant B to do his allotted share of the job. If B likes cleaning and is good at it, and has no opportunity to put his talents to work productively in other ways, both A and B would be better off with a rule permitting substitution.

As occupational specialization rises, the more 'allocatively' wasteful doing-it-yourself becomes, in principle. For instance, it was common in many countries in the past (and still applies in a few places today) to organize road maintenance by obliging all able-bodied adult males to take part in the job for a few days each year. Such an arrangement is less wasteful in a community in which most males work on general farming tasks, especially when slack times in the agricultural cycle make it possible to do other work without much sacrifice, than it would be in a community of highly diverse and non-seasonal specializations.

Equally, allocative waste from compelling direct and non-substitutable part-time performance of a service by users will be greater the more the task lends itself to performance by highly specialized equipment. This certainly applies to road repair today (see Dunsire, 1973, p. 191). Applying the traditional method of organizing road maintenance in today's urban communities might well be fun. But the allocative waste created by the general farm worker of 200 years ago wielding a pick and shovel on the roads during the dead of winter would be as nothing compared to that which would be created by making, say, a modern brain surgeon fumble inexpertly with a modern road-mending machine for a few days in his working year (perhaps actually causing net damage as a result of his inexperience and lack of skill). Exactly the same might be said about the organization of fire services, traffic control, and so on.

This is, so it is conventionally argued, the reason for the relative decline of in-kind or do-it-yourself provision of public services in modern societies. But this mode of organization has not disappeared entirely. In large-scale disasters or emergencies, for instance (when, by definition, normal systems of values do not operate), there may be no alternative to pressing into service whatever labour and equipment is available on the spot.

Moreover, for some public services, strict task specialization may even be rejected as a matter of policy. For example, compelling part-time military service by everyone might be seen as a way to avoid what might otherwise be a dangerous conflict of interest between a full-time military corps and the civilian population – and thus to reduce the risk of military *coups*, and the like. Or it might be held to be desirable in principle for all citizens to take part in the administration of justice through jury service, rather than for professional full-time magistrates to do the job alone.

For other reasons too, many public services are organized on the basis of some degree of compulsory co-production by users. Efforts to cut costs both in private and public services often involve increasing the degree of self-service, in matters such as exact-fare buses and tolls, self-read domestic utility metering, and the like. In Tokyo, customers do part of the job of sorting domestic garbage, by an obligation to place garbage of different types in specific containers (e.g. glass, paper, batteries, burnable and non-burnable items). Obliging user cooperation in the production of the service in cases like this is not likely to create an allocative waste problem of very serious dimensions, especially when it is set against the potential inefficiences bound up with using specialists through employment or performance contracts, to be considered below.

It may well be that advocating total 'do-it-yourself' in service provision is naive and utopian, and that Illich and others may have exaggerated the negative effects of specialization in service provision. But doing-it-yourself is always an option in service provision. It is usually a matter of more or less rather than all or nothing. Very few services are provided without any 'co-production' at all.

III. SCALE OF ORGANIZATION

Scale of organization is closely linked to specialization in practice. Long ago, Adam Smith pointed out that the scope for specialization usually depends on the number of customers to be served. In our apartment block cleaning example, if each block hires its own cleaner, each cleaner must tackle all kinds of cleaning work. If organization is on the scale of apartment blocks throughout the city, there can be specialists at no extra cost to each tenant – for instance in window cleaning, floor polishing, and so on. The question is, of course, at what point in the provision of a service are the specialization advantages of increasing scale exhausted or outweighed by corresponding disadvantages, for instance in extra difficulties in coordination and control?

Public services in practice are organized at many different levels of scale. They vary from the apartment block scale to the transnational scale of provision. Many public services do not fit neatly within the boundaries of a particular state. Indeed, in principle, there could be international trade in public services in the same way as any other commodity, with similar potential advantages from concentrating provision in the hands of least-cost suppliers. This is rarely taken very far in practice. But diminutives of it (in the shape of agency agreements, and the like) are not at all uncommon.

What criteria might govern choices about the scale on which any particular public service might be provided? Consider three possible criteria, which to some degree overlap with one another:

(a)   The scale of public good involved in a service;
(b)   the impact of scale on efficiency of operations;
(c)   the community of consumers to which the service in question is intended to be primarily responsive or accessible.

First, the scale of public good involved in a service. If service organization does not match exactly the scale of public good, transactions costs will arise in providing service. Transactions costs are the cost of reaching and/or enforcing agreements, fixing rules, writing contracts (see Chapter 1). Where public or joint-consumption goods are in question, some such costs must necessarily be incurred before service can be provided, as we have seen.

Public goods, as we saw in Chapter 1, can come at many different levels of scale. Keeping the common parts of an apartment building clean is a mini-public good restricted to a fairly small number of beneficiaries. The same goes for flood control in V, as described in Chapter 1. At the other end of the scale from the apartment cleaning case, the control of acid rain appears to be a maxi-public good, of continental dimensions.

To the extent that the boundaries of institutions responsible for organizing provision follow the scale of the public good in question, the less will be the transactions which must be entered into with other institutions to provide the good. *Per contra*, the less that jurisdictional boundaries of institutions reflect the scale of public goods, the more inter-institutional transactions will be needed to provide the good.

Let us go back to the case of V for an example. Suppose that there is an exactly similar village, W, on the *right* bank of R, at M. Suppose that V and W each has a village council armed with public power to raise taxes, and the like. Further, suppose that, if M is blocked, the chances of R seeking a new mouth to the right of M are no more and no less than the chances of it going to the left of M. That means that each village stands equally to gain from stabilizing M, and faces the same downside risk. The physical problem and the public good bound up with it are exactly as in Chapter 1, except that now two autonomous villages are affected rather than one.

Obviously, there are strategic problems inherent in this situation. The council and taxpayers of each village might very naturally want to free-ride collectively, leaving it to the other village to take the necessary action and shoulder the costs. The attendant risk, of course, is that the flood-control works will be under-provided or not provided at all – the 'tragedy of the commons' in a slightly different guise. Alternatively, if both V and W act to control M, the works may be duplicated or over-provided. Worse, the actions of each village might be pitted against those of the other, in that V might undertake works to push R's mouth to the right of M, while W simultaneously carried out works to push R's mouth to the left of M. Stranger things have been known to happen.

In such circumstances, there may well be advantages in organizing services on a scale which includes both V and W. For instance, the villages might take it in turns to provide the services, on an annual (or other) basis. Alternatively, an enterprise operating for both V and W might be set up to carry out the works on the basis of taxes raised from both settlements, either under joint management or operated by one of the villages on an agency basis for the other.

Fitting the scale of organization to the scale of the relevant public good so as to limit transactions costs looks like a clear-cut principle. It often comes into administrative arguments. But the boundaries of public goods are often so fuzzy that in practice this is a vaguer design principle than it seems at first sight. Even in the case of V, the beneficiaries from flood control may be hard to identify at the margin. Obviously, the village's permanent residents stand to benefit. But what about people who come from the hinterland to V to work, or trade with V, as in the case of the lumber enterprises upstream on R? The economy of the whole country – even, perhaps, the world – might be to some infinitesimal degree impoverished if V is destroyed. Where exactly do the boundaries of flood prevention as a public good lie? When it comes to settling the limits of the necessary tax base, this is not just an academic question.

Second, the impact of scale on operational efficiency. One of the classic themes in social science is the idea that the scale on which production is organized can affect the efficiency with which inputs are converted into outputs. Average costs of production may depend on the total amount produced. The *locus classicus*, mentioned at the start of this section, is Adam Smith's discussion of the way that an expansion of clientele increases the scope for division of labour and hence, in many circumstances, for greater productive efficiency (Smith, 1978, pp. 86–5, 564–5). Analogous arguments have been advanced for specifically administrative services (see Dunsire, 1973, pp. 189–93). Small settlements like V, for instance, will usually find it disproportionately expensive to operate their own electricity plant or prisons.

In fact, studies of scale economies are few. Such as there are, even in manufacturing industry (such as Stigler, 1958), tend to reveal a wide range of optimum sizes, not a single best size. The same goes for specifically public services (see Wildavsky, 1979, p. 151). Lack of clear evidence for scale economies in production has tended to cause advocates of large-scale organization in industry to shift their ground to the idea that bigger scale brings inherent advantages in research and innovation. Even this claim is hard to substantiate (Jewkes *et al.*, 1969, p. 186). But the general argument remains influential.

On the other hand, it is conventionally assumed that as scale of enterprise rises, the cost and difficulty of controlling the enterprise will start to rise sharply at some point. (Indeed, Niskanen (in Weiss and Barton, 1980, p. 171) claims that when it comes to public bureaucracies, production efficiency is always negatively linked to scale of coverage.) At least at some point the average costs of production start to *rise* with the total amount produced. The upper limit on the efficient size of enterprises will depend on the point at which control costs 'take off' (see Jackson, 1982, pp. 178–84). Moreover, the consequences of mistakes made by large enterprises are likely to be more serious than mistakes made by small ones, and making changes in large enterprises is apt to be a cumbersome, laborious, traumatic and crisis-ridden process.

There are thus potentially opposed factors to be balanced, to find the scale of production at which average production costs are lowest. Often this turns out to be a matter of nice and subjective judgement, since many factors, many of them intangible (morale, social discipline, and the like) can affect control costs in most cases. This criterion, too, is much fuzzier in practice than it seems at first sight.

We can go back to the case of V to illustrate this argument. Suppose that, taking one year with another, it takes 10 man-days per year to do the work of stabilizing M. However, 20 years may pass without any work needed at all. Then, unpredictably and at short notice, 200 man-days may be needed. This is a familiar problem. If V maintains special-purpose capacity to stabilize M, the resources will be idle most of the time and will be in that sense wasted unless they can be put to other uses while they are standing by – something that tends to be less possible the more specialized the machinery or people are. Alternatively, if extra hands are hired, volunteers drummed up or available equipment obtained only when and if M starts to block up, the hands are likely to be unused to the work, the equipment unfamiliar or not precisely suited to the job, causing delays, hitches, false starts, misunderstandings, of a kind which come from lack of specialization (see section II above).

Now if there are several villages facing more or less the same river mouth problem as V, an enterprise common to all of them will be less prone to the problems which a V-specific enterprise would face, in terms of under-used specialized resources or inefficient under-specialization. Potentially, organizing on the larger scale combines financial benefits of spreading risks (through a larger insurance pool) with production benefits associated with extra specialization.

That is, assuming that not all of these villages would normally face crisis at once (on account of differences in location and weather zones, say), such an enterprise could operate throughout the year with proportionately less idle time than would a V-specific enterprise. It could fully employ specialized staff and equipment which would be very costly to set aside for work on M alone – for instance, computer modellers of river mouth dynamics, underwater blasting experts, aero-reconnaissance for monitoring changes, satellite-based weather forecasting operations, and the like. It is not that V could not have its own weather satellite or river mouth dynamics research station (or, indeed, its own prison and power plant); only that the costs of such specialized apparatus will be lower per unit the larger the clientele which it serves, and that (within *some* range, at least) specialization may itself reduce unit costs (see Dunsire, 1973, pp. 188–93).

Clearly scale of clientele potentially affects production effeciency in such cases. In principle the design problem is to set the scale of organization at the point where extra productive efficiency from full-time specialization more than offsets higher direction costs arising from an increase in scale of operation. Technical-seeming references to 'economies of scale' often figure large in debate about scale of public service organization. But such arguments should be looked at carefully, given the difficulty of finding the 'best scale' point in practice.

For instance, what are asserted to be economies of scale in administration all too often turn out to be no more than devices for shifting costs from producer to consumer, frequently by a move towards increased self-help (Ostrom, 1974, p. 61; Sharpe, 1986, p. 175). Suppose that two areas formerly served by two service outlets are replaced by a single outlet of the same capacity as one of the two previous ones, but only open for half the time. What is really taking place is a cut in service quality (customers must wait four times as long for service), not a rise in productive efficiency. Yet changes like this often masquerade as economies of scale. *True* economies of scale arise only when the same service can be produced more cheaply on a larger than a smaller scale, or when a better service can be offered for the same cost. We shall return to the issue of shifting costs between producer and consumer in Chapter 6.

The third scale of organization criterion is to base service on the community of users to which the service in question is intended to be primarily responsive. This is a non-technical criterion, taking appropriate scale from a politically-defined community of beneficiaries, irrespective of arguments about transactions costs or production efficiency. Indeed, it begins with the consumers rather than the producers. This is a cruder-seeming criterion than the two discussed so far. But it is often more robust, given the imponderables typically associated with putting the other two into practice, for all that those may initially appear more 'scientific'.

For the organization of any service, there is more than an abstract possibility that these criteria will conflict with one another. In the flood control case, it might well be that a combination of villages V and W turn out to be the scale of organization which minimizes transactions costs for stabilizing M. But a larger group of river mouth villages (X, Y and Z, as well as V and W) might be the maximum production-efficiency scale of operations. At the same time, it might be that V's residents strongly desire to base service organization on V and V alone, so as to keep lines from producers to consumers as short as possible. They might want that in the belief that accessibility to clients or democratic responsiveness is inversely related to scale of operations (the larger the scale of enterprise, the more remote leaders become and the harder it is for outsiders to exert influence). Which criterion of scale is to prevail in such a case?

The first two criteria for scale of organization both lead us to prefer that each public service be organized on a different scale, suited to its own special features. But the third criterion may lead us to want all services organized on the *same* scale: the classic case for general-purpose local (or national) government, in fact. In principle, when scale of organization is at issue, the merits of *each* criterion should be argued through systematically. All too often in practice, one criterion comes to dominate the case by default.

One way of resolving the potential conflicts among these criteria is to overlay enterprises representing each one of them into a network. For instance, there could be a general-purpose representative institution for V entering for convenience into a formal agreement with a similar institution for W to agree jointly a deal with a third enterprise, operating on a different scale. This raises the issue of whether public services should involve single-enterprise or multi-enterprise providers, and we shall come to that in section V.

IV. PERFORMANCE CONTRACTS VERSUS EMPLOYMENT

(1) The Performance Contract Problem
A third choice in organization is whether to work through specific performance contracts or through direct employment. In the apartment-cleaning case, the tenants might directly employ a cleaner or might enter into specific performance contracts laying down price, period, quantity and/or quality of all the work needed to clean the building (see Posner, 1977, p. 289).

This choice potentially applies to any public service. Often, it is a matter of choosing a *mix* of direct employment and performance contracts rather than a case of either/or. One way of exploring the contract employment issue is to compare the costs and difficulties arising in each mode of provision. In a now classic analysis on these lines, Williamson (1975) suggests

that factors likely to lead to the use of direct employment rather than performance contracts are:
(a) *uncertainty*, paired with *limited rationality*; and
(b) *small numbers* of parties to a transaction, paired with *opportunism*.

First, the more uncertain or complex (interrelated) a task is, the harder it becomes to draw up contracts to cover all the contingencies which may conceivably arise. In the case of V, for instance, the remedial action needed for flood control might depend on the precise conditions of tide, wind, the water level of R and/or L, the configuration of M. Some floods might be limited or prevented by careful monitoring – for example of obstructions building up at M. But in other cases (as is often the way with floods) trouble might come unpredictably, so that all that can be done is to limit the damage after it has occurred. Writing a contract to take account of these contingencies in specifying the performance standard required of a contractor might well be tricky, certainly costly in time and effort, perhaps simply impossible. No two floods are quite the same. At some point the cost faced by those responsible for framing and negotiating such a contract might exceed the costs of managing employees. An employee can be directed to deal with problems as they happen, in the way that seems most appropriate at the time, but an enforceable contract must take care of all the contingencies in advance. It is the 'laws not men' problem in a different guise.

Williamson pairs uncertainty with limited rationality, because uncertainty is only a 'problem' in framing contracts if there are limits to our capacity to identify all the possible contingencies that may arise, assign probabilities to each of them and specify what should be done in each contingency. Equally, limited rationality is only a problem to the extent that the future is uncertain.

Uncertainty and limited rationality, of course, figure large in many public services. Many jobs which are typically done by direct public service employees, do indeed involve high uncertainty. There are many contingencies which it would be very laborious to provide for in advance by specific contracts – for instance, military operations, diplomacy, policing, currency management. Circumstances in such spheres change from day to day, even from minute to minute. The nature of the task cannot easily be specified in advance, especially as regards quality of work (this is the classic problem with hiring mercenary soldiers, of course). On the other hand, for work like street cleaning, night-soil removal, power supply, transport services, there is less uncertainty and it is easier to specify quality of performance and how the job is to be done, which may be why such services are very often *not* provided by direct public service employees.

Second, the fewer the buyers and/or sellers involved, the less is likely to be the advantage of using performance contracts rather than employment. Where there are many sellers and many buyers, the process of completing transactions will tend to be simplified and standardized. If there are 100 contract-cleaning firms among whom the tenants in the apartment block case can choose, it will probably be easier to negotiate a deal than it would be if there was only one such firm. In the extreme case where a single seller confronts a single buyer, it is likely to be very difficult to agree a deal, with a high probability of deadlock, and extended haggling over performance clauses. An employment contract, once agreed, may reduce these difficulties. Command is substituted for prior agreement among contracting parties on every particular. Instead of resolving disputes over the interpretation of performance clauses in court or by legal negotiations, moral pressure, informal evidence, and the like may be brought to bear.

Williamson pairs small numbers with opportunism, because small numbers in negotiation only become a 'problem' in making transactions to the extent that negotiators act strategically and self-regardingly, exploiting each situation for maximum personal advantage. Equally, opportunism is only a problem where small-numbers transactions take place, because in a market with many buyers and sellers, the scope for the exercise of opportunism by any one participant is likely to be fairly small.

This, too, has implications for public service organization. Where there is only one possible supplier – for instance, in a non-contestable market, like the piped-water supply for V – or where numbers of suppliers are small for other reasons, the inherent advantage of performance contracting over direct employment is far from clear-cut. Where public services are performed on contract by a monopoly enterprise or by a cartel, the service cannot be turned over to other suppliers either simultaneously or successively. This form of organization has the advantage neither of the direct employment relation nor of the contract form.

This is what happened to tax collection in Europe in the seventeenth and eighteenth centuries. A competitive private franchise system for tax collection turned into *de facto* monopolies which were in turn supplanted by direct employment of tax collectors by government. Even Adam Smith, who is usually taken to be the classic totem of 'free enterprise', stressed the limitations of contracting in such a case. He preferred the British system of direct employment of tax collectors on fixed salaries to the French system of auctioning the right to collect taxes to the highest bidder. In the latter case, he said, less than half of the money raised in taxes was paid to the government. The reason was that

in an auction of this kind there are few bidders, as none are capable of undertaking the office but those who are brought up to business, and are possessed both of a great stock and credit, and can produce good security. When there are few bidders [i.e. the small-numbers problem] they can easily enter into an association among themselves and have the whole at a very easy rate (Smith, 1978, p. 534).

Similar issues are raised today in many spheres of public contracting.

Table 4.1: Uncertainty and small-numbers exchange relations: Examples

| Uncertainty | Numbers involved in exchange relations (i.e. number of suppliers, number of consumers, or both) | |
	Inherently small	Potentially large
Inherently high	Diplomatic representation services	Economic forecasting Labour-dispute conciliation
Potentially low	Supply of piped water	Provision of general practitioner medical services

Hence, even if one starts with a strong bias *against* direct employment for providing public services, it is hard to avoid running up against a *prima facie* case for such organization in circumstances where public services combine high uncertainty and inherently small numbers of suppliers. Table 4.1 summarizes this argument. Diplomacy, for instance, combines high uncertainty with a limited number of possible suppliers of the service: unpromising ground for performance contracting. On the other hand, where there is greater certainty as to how the job should be done and potentially large numbers of rival providers (as in schools and general medical practitioner services), a stronger *prima facie* case for specific contracts in service provision might be made. It is in situations cutting across these categories that the argument becomes less clear-cut – for instance, where high uncertainty combines with potentially large numbers of competitors, as with economic forecasting or labour dispute conciliation. It is in such areas that one might expect to see more hybrid forms of organization.

(2) Direct Employment: The Servant Problem

So far, we have looked at the possible problems involved in negotiating performance contracts. Now consider the other side of the picture: the cost and difficulty of the master–servant relationship. This includes: costs of hiring, grading, promoting and firing staff; costs of negotiating pay, allowances, funds for materials and equipment; costs of overseeing employees so as to limit organizational slack (as mentioned in the last chapter), i.e. to keep under-employed, unemployed or misused resources at an acceptable level. Servants may be idle. Equipment may be incompetently used. Lack of motivation may prevent resources from reaching the output of which they are physically capable. Adam Smith thought such problems were inherent in large-scale employment relations, and based his opposition to joint stock companies on the grounds that separation of ownership and management destroys the incentive for 'unremitting exertion of vigilance and attention' (Rosenberg, 1960, p. 563).

This kind of efficiency is different from allocative efficiency, as discussed in section II. Organizational slack – the failure to work as hard or effectively as we could, with given equipment and resources – is often referred to as X-inefficiency, to distinguish it from allocative inefficiency (cf. Leibenstein, 1976). It is central to the management of the 'servant problem'.

The 'servant problem' starts with the first employee. Obviously, it figures large where employment is on a large scale. Until modern times, controlling a mass of employees was a problem affecting only imperial, military and ecclesiastical organization. Perhaps for that reason, classical economics said little about the 'servant problem'. It followed the law in treating corporate enterprises as individuals – a fiction that was not unreasonable at a time when most firms were small (see Jackson, 1982, pp. 46–83). Moreover, it assumed that a competitive industry structure would take care of the servant problem one way or another. Enterprises which were least successful in managing their employees so as to limit slack would come to be eliminated by the market. Those assumptions never applied without major exceptions to public service organization, and became shakier even in the ordinary economic sphere with the advent of giant corporations.

The 'servant problem' is potentially aggravated:

(a) When an enterprise pluralizes its operations across territory – for example, a college which operates in separate campuses, a bus company which sets up a chain of depots, a police force which divides up into police posts or stations. (On 'pluralization', see Kochen and Deutsch, 1980, p. 33ff; Rose, 1985, p. 7.) The familiar problem of conflict or misunderstanding between employees in the field and the central directorate then starts to appear.

(b) When, with or without pluralization, an enterprise comes to employ many specialists of different types, pursuing different purposes: the college with many faculties, the bus company with experts in finance, marketing, engineering, personnel management, customer relations, the police force with specialists in criminal records, computer crime, commercial crime, arson, community relations.

The more servants there are, the more physically scattered they are, the more divided they are into recondite specialisms, the greater the dimensions of the slack-control problem become.

Williamson (1975, p. 15) uses the term 'information-impactedness' to denote a situation in which information required by a master to evaluate the behaviour of a servant is monopolized to some degree by that servant. How is the master (who might be a collectivity of consumers, as in the apartment cleaning case) to discover and check the degree of slack in the work of servants?

Information-impactedness only becomes a problem when it is compounded with discretion and opportunism. Discretion by servants or agents (on how to act, on what information to pass to masters or principals) is inescapably bound up with information-impactedness. A huge and diverse literature addresses the problem of discretionary behaviour by employees (see Jackson, 1982, p. 182). Discretion itself is potentially a 'problem' only to the extent that it is used opportunistically: that is, if servants act self-regardingly, following their own personal interests, rather than in a fiduciary or altruistic fashion.

What happens when information-impactedness combines with opportunism on the part of the servant? Conventionally, the argument goes that the servant will filter information to the master in ways that reflect the interests of the former rather than the latter. News about efficiency, successes or likely future successes will be exaggerated and amplified. News about waste and failure will be muted, played down, filtered out. The master may thus be led into serious errors as a result of deciding or acting on false assumptions and distorted information (Tullock, 1965). Slack on the part of subordinates will be hard to detect.

That problem in turn will tend to be more severe:
- (a) the greater the degree of monopoly built into the servant's position;
- (b) the greater the number of authority levels in an enterprise; and
- (c) the less measurable the servant's output.

Obviously, the more monopolistic is the servant's position *vis-à-vis* the master, the greater the potential information-impactedness and hence the scope for discretion linked to opportunistic distortion of information. Such monopoly may relate to a place or to a skill or specialism (for instance, only the fingerprinting division knows how many fingerprinting experts are needed to handle demand without slack). If the employing enterprise is itself a monopoly, a monopoly unit within it will have few effective checks on slack and information distortion. Indeed, power within enterprises typically depends on the ability to monopolize key functions (see, for instance, Crozier, 1964). This small-numbers problem is, as was mentioned earlier, one of the possible reasons for organizing work on the basis of direct employment rather than by contracting for specific services. But the problem by no means disappears once it has been internalized into a direct employment relationship.

Second, the longer the hierarchical chain of authority in an enterprise, the more scope for information distortion is likely to exist. The problem of 'diminishing control' in hierarchies figured large in the bureaucratic behaviour theories of Tullock (1965) and Downs (1967) in the 1960s, although the problem of hierarchical information distortion in general was well known to scholars of an earlier generation (see von Mises, 1944; Simon, Smithburg and Thompson, 1950, pp. 236–40). There are at least three ways in which information may be distorted in a subordinate–superordinate relationship. Each type of distortion is likely to rise with the number of hierarchical levels in an enterprise:

(a) Self-interested distortion of information by a servant to his master, as discussed earlier. Suppose that the proportion of the 'total picture' (whatever that is) which is distorted for this reason at any level of the hierarchy is given as:

a_1

(b) 'Natural' (i.e. unintended) distortion of information due to error. It is a commonplace of story-telling games or 'whispering' experiments that unintended error steadily creeps into a message as it passes from one person to another, especially if transmitted by word of mouth alone. This kind of distortion is likely to be most serious when employees are physically scattered, when they possess a diversity of specialized skills such that information must be repeatedly translated from technical into lay language and back, or when action may have to take place very fast, for instance on the basis of telephone messages rather than written reports. Suppose that the proportion of the 'total picture' distorted for this reason at any level of the hierarchy is given as:

b_1

(c) Distortion arising from deliberate simplification of messages as they travel upwards in a hierarchy, or bulking out messages as they travel downwards. Dunsire (1980, pp. 37–8) has shown that, even if there is no self-interested distortion whatever on the part of servants, some distortion is bound to arise simply because of the functional need to cut down on the detail known to a servant in order to convey the 'bottom line' of a situation to a busy master with other things on his mind and a finite capacity to absorb and process information. Similarly, when a message goes down from the top, 'implied terms' must be progressively introduced in order to convey its practical meaning in terms of work routines and the like. Call the proportion of the total picture distorted for this reason at any level of the hierarchy:

c_1

The proportion of any message distorted (L) as it crosses any level in an enterprise's hierarchy is then:

$$(1 - [a_1 + b_1 + c_1]).$$

L will grow larger the more levels there are in the hierarchy. If there are n levels, the total distortion of any message as it passes from the bottom of the enterprise to the top will be:

$$(1 - [a_1 + b_1 + c_1])^{n-1}$$

(This is a modified version of a formula put forward by Breton, 1974.)

Even if one makes conservative assumptions about what values to attach to each of these three distortion factors, the cumulative effects are potentially dramatic in long hierarchies. For instance, if the proportion of the total picture distorted by each of these three factors is 0.1 at each stage (little enough, it may be agreed), it only takes a three-level hierarchy for the distortion factor to climb above half of the total message conveyed, so that the picture which gets to the top is more wrong than right. If accurate decision-making at the top requires the combination of several separate messages, the likelihood that the enterprise directorate will *ever* make any correct decisions becomes very low (see Beer, 1966, pp. 196–7).

Third, the scope for information distortion and discretionary behaviour by the servant will tend to increase, the less readily measurable is the quality and quantity of output. That scope will be large if the product is intangible or its quality is hard to assess (as with medical care), if there are potentially conflicting evaluation criteria (e.g. procedure versus results) or if success or failure by an employee may be caused by hard to disentangle multiple outputs from more than one person or office.

Each of these problems, taken on its own, is serious enough. When all three come together, the information distortion problem may become dramatic. Bennett (1983, p. 19) describes the way that a 'fantasy factor' can creep in to large-scale computer projects. Turner (1976, pp. 57–8) puts distortion at the top of a list of factors which cause large-scale disasters.

It follows that there are broadly three strategies which can be used to counter the discretionary behaviour/information distortion problem in large-scale master–servant organization;
(1) Seek to reduce opportunism.
(2) Seek to limit discretion.
(3) Fix the rules of the game such that opportunism and discretion produce positive rather than negative results: in other words, changing the *consequences* of opportunism and discretion.

(1) Limiting Opportunism
We have already seen that discretionary behaviour and information-impactedness within a master–servant relationship is a 'problem' only if the servants are opportunistic. So one way of tackling the problem at the root is by trying to limit opportunism, making servants act as fiduciaries (acting solely for the benefit of their master) rather than looking after Number One. Such an approach can hardly· be avoided where servants are to be sent out to far-flung districts where the exercise of discretion, local monopoly and

information-impactedness is unavoidable, as in the case of missionaries, spies, colonial administrators. Traditional public administration theory emphasizes this approach, seeking to put the running of public services in the hands of people not subject to worldly corruption – sometimes with explicit comparison to a priesthood (Niskanen, 1971, p. 192). Schaffer (1973, p. 39) quotes a dictum by Sir Arthur Helps in this vein: 'There should be men in office who love the state as priests love the church.' Indeed, the quasi-religious idea of public service employment as a 'calling' has been linked with substantive religious ideas in several of the great bureaucratic societies of the past (such as Confucianism in Imperial China, Protestantism and Freemasonry in Imperial Prussia).

Conventional means used to limit opportunism by employees include the following, none of which is foolproof and many of which overlap:

(a) Accepting as employees only people who show signs of vocation or permanent calling to the work in question, as tested by rigorous scrutiny, screening and probation procedures, not casual job-hoppers momentarily attracted to the pay or the job.

(b) Lifetime career service (another facet of 'vocation'). This may encourage people to take a 'long view' which may limit opportunism, especially if allied to more or less automatic progression by seniority and 'cradle to grave' benefits from the employer. Just as those who regularly deal with one another in trade have more reason to act honestly than those who interact only in discrete or one-off transactions, employees who must work with one another in a group for decades before they get pensions or promotion cannot easily indulge in fly-by-night tactics of getting rich quick and then moving on to something else.

(c) Long induction and training procedures, to cultivate a sense of enterprise solidarity and to limit the grosser aspects of self-serving behaviour. This is, for instance, the intended purpose of the rule that English lawyers eat a stipulated number of dinners at an Inn of Court before becoming barristers, so that they absorb the atmosphere and ethics of the legal profession and become socially involved with their peers, rather than merely studying the law in the books.

(2) Limiting Discretion

Whereas the 'priesthood' approach aims to tackle the servant problem by limiting opportunism, a logically opposite approach is to accept opportunism but limit discretion. This is, of course, a rule design problem and harks back to the discussion of minimal discretion rules in Chapter 2. Organization theorists conventionally use the term formalization to denote the degree to which enterprises govern their affairs by explicit formal rules for the conduct of business, reporting requirements, authorization and appeal procedures to check and limit the discretion of agents, closely specified performance targets. As with 'laws not men' rules more generally, it has often been noted that the more formalized the operations of an enterprise are, the more decentralized it can be (Perrow, 1979). This is because the formal rules are intended to limit discretion and stop servants from turning their office to private advantage. The logical development of this approach (as with minimal discretion rules in general) is the automated factory or office, in which the rules are physically programmed into the structure.

(3) Harnessing Discretion and Opportunism

Tackling the servant problem at source – either by limiting discretion or damping down opportunism – is not without its drawbacks. In principle, discretion has many advantages, as we saw in the last chapter in comparing a rule enforcement machine with discretionary rule enforcement. Too many rules can be stultifying. Notoriously, strictly defined output targets such as distance driven by police cars or number of traffic tickets issued will distort performance, causing statistics to be created for the record without regard for the real value of such activities (Ostrom, 1981, p. 45). Damping down opportunistic tendencies by servants may have negative side-effects, too. It may exchange competence for loyalty, effectiveness for honesty, independent thought for groupthink, analytic capacity for piety, capability for seniority. It may mean being too kind to employees with burnout, declining competence, skill obsolescence (or who are just plain failures) – in short, to do without all the potentially benefits of opportunism, in terms of dynamism, quick-wittedness, adaptivity. Such approaches tend to kill (or at least weaken) the patient as well as curing the disease.

An alternative approach is to take both opportunism and discretion by servants for granted, but to devise a rule structure such that these forces produce positive rather than negative results. Among the many devices which build on this general approach are the limitation of tenure, the creation of cross-cutting structures, the creation of league tables and the engineering of payment on performance.

(1) *Limit Tenure.* One of the traditional ways of harnessing opportunism and discretion is to give servants only limited or conditional tenure. The servant's continuance or advancement in office is made to depend on the fortunes or approval of the master. If this can be done, the servant's interest is unavoidably linked to that of the master, so discretion and opportunism on the part of the former automatically works for the latter. This is, of course, completely different from limiting opportunism by lifetime career structures. Many rulers, from earliest times to the present day, have tried to obtain loyalty by drawing their servants from people without independent resources or authority (outsiders, aliens, people of low esteem), so that the careers of those agents cannot continue to prosper if their principal's fortunes sink.

(2) *Cross-Cutting Structures.* Downs' (1967) 'Law of Control Duplication' says that if you want to control one large bureaucracy, you must create another. Flippant as this may seem, it has sound intellectual underpinnings. 'Control' is conventionally defined in control theory as the capacity to keep the state of a system within some sub-set of all its possible states, such that the state of the system can be changed at any time. (This may seem rather abstract: think what it means, say, for driving a car.) Ashby's (1956) 'Law of Requisite Variety' says that control in this sense can exist only to the extent that the number of states that the controller can take up at least matches the number of states that the object of control can take

up (the driver must have a response to every state that the car may get into). This is the logic of developing large audit offices, 'second guessing' institutions, adversary bureaucracies, duplication and rivalry within employment enterprises. In Chapter 2 we saw that contradictions may come into rules and criteria in order to give power to adjudicators. Rival opportunists with stakes in different rules will conflict, such that 'outside' resolution will be needed.

Thus, both economics-bases and cybernetics-based ideas about large enterprises stress the need for 'redundancy' (duplication, overlap, competition) and built-in conflict to keep such enterprises under control. This applies especially to enterprises which do not compete in a market and thus run little risk of being driven out of business – meaning that there is no inherent congruence of interest between master and servant. This 'cross-cutting structures' approach conflicts sharply with a style of thinking about administrative organization which seeks to minimize duplication, conflict and overlap. We shall come back to this issue in the next section.

(3) *League Tables and Competing Teams.* A particular application of the cross-cutting structures approach is what Williamson (1975, p. 159) calls 'capitalism's creative response' to the problems of self-regarding discretionary behaviour and information distortion within large corporations. This approach began to be applied within General Motors and Du Pont in the 1920s. It involves:

(a) 'Double-sourcing' (avoiding dependency on any one single plant for important products or services, usually by running duplicate plants in different countries); and

(b) changing from what Williamson terms a unitary-form enterprise (that is, one with an unbroken hierarchical chain of command from top to bottom) to a multi-divisional form of enterprise (M-form).

M-form enterprises consist of competing plants constituted as quasi-enterprises – that is, trading with one another on a charging basis, competing in a league and operating with independent profit-and-loss accounts. This means that the plants are in continuous rivalry and that relationships among them are expressed in quasi-contracts specifying performance standards. The top directorate ceases to exercise close supervision in an unbroken chain of hierarchical command reaching into every nook of the enterprise (with all the distortion of information problems that such a structure invites in a large enterprise). Instead, it acts as a holding company or merchant bank, allocating capital to individual sub-companies in the light of rival bids for capital or profit performance, promoting or firing managers on the same basis. The enterprise becomes a mini-industry, building redundancy and duplication into its plant structure.

(4) *Payment on Performance*. Discretion and opportunism may be harnessed by linking employee rewards to performance, as with commission fees, piece rates, stock options. A specific performance contract is laid on top of an employment contract. If an employee's reward comes from a fixed salary alone, he or she cannot benefit from saving costs or raising output, nor suffer from failure to do so. Any gains to the employee of cost-saving, innovation, increased output, can only come in the form of promotions and pay raises, but such processes tend to work very creakily or not at all in mass-employment enterprises. Thus if fixed-salary employees are opportunistic, they have little incentive to raise output or cut costs. Adam Smith (1937, p. 678) drew the moral that 'Public services are never better performed than when their [public officials'] reward comes only in consequence of their being performed, and is proportionate to the diligence employed in performing them'.

In section VI, we shall look at the implications of this well-known dictum for the financing of public services. In the present context, it shows Smith's concern with building performance-based incentive structures into the employment relation for those conditions where he thought employment produced better results than contracting. Smith, as a college professor, contrasted what he saw as the superior educational service offered by the public schools of that day (whose teachers were paid from student fees) with that of the universities (whose teachers were paid out of endowment funds to a large degree). He noted that in the richer and best-endowed universities, teachers (a) formed the governing body; (b) drew their salaries from endowments; and (c) compelled students to attend classes.

These institutions were, he argued, the most producer-dominated and unresponsive to student demand, combining 'contemptuous and arrogant airs' with negligence and sloth in the performance of duties (cf. Rosenberg, 1960, pp. 568–9; Ostrom, 1982, pp. 11–12).

Performance-related reward systems raise exactly the same problem in practice as setting measurable output targets in a rule structure designed to limit discretion – namely that opportunists produce the right statistics for the record, whether or not that reflects high-quality work. If academics are rewarded by number of words written, pitiless verbosity is the inevitable result. If architects or other professionals are rewarded by 'scale fees' (a share of the final cost of projects), the incentives are to push project costs up as far as possible rather than to aim for savings. Output-linked rewards can easily be perverse. But such incentives were widely used in public service organization before the rise of fixed-salary employment in public bureaucracies over the past century. Some officials were rewarded in part at least for money that they saved from the sums budgeted, as in the old system of tax-farming, or military supply by colonels and muster-men (Niskanen, 1971, p. 194). Others were paid according to the quality of service they provided, as in the case of dis-covery of contraband by customs officials. Fixed salaries are not the only way of rewarding employees in a master–servant relationship.

These four approaches do not exhaust the possibilities. They merely show some possible ways of designing institutional structures so that employees' opportunism and discretion can be led to produce positive effects. They all reflect the view that (to modify another dictum of Adam Smith) it is not from the benevolence or altruism of employees that we must normally expect public services to be provided, but from their pursuit of self-interest. Just as production is a by-product of pursuit of profit in a market, so the provision of services by employees is incidental to the pursuit of self-interest by those employees (see Schumpeter, 1954, p. 282). Hence, from this point of view, the problem is to find a way to anchor the servant's pursuit of self-interest with the interest of the master without destroying either opportunism or discretion.

Figure 4.2 summarizes the broad options for addressing the 'servant problem' which have been discussed here – i.e. limiting discretion, limiting opportunism, channelling discretion and opportunism. Option 4 on Figure 4.2 is an empty box – logically possible, but redundant. If opportunism is very low, you don't need to limit discretion, and vice versa. Options 2 and 3 in their extreme form are incompatible with option 1, so that combinations are feasible only if any one option is less than fully successful. Even then, trying to combine them may well produce confusion or worse (lifetime career and seniority promotion versus conditional tenure and performance-related rewards, for instance). We can't have it all ways in this case.

Table 4.2: Handling the servant problem: Strategies

		Keep opportunism: High	Low
Keep discretion	*High*	1. Harnessed opportunistic discretion	2. Selfless or fiduciary servant
	Low	3. Red tape	4. Rule-bound altruism

V. SINGLE PROVIDER OR MULTIPLE PROVIDERS?

A fourth choice in organization is whether to provide service through one monopoly producer, or to use multiple producers. If the second is chosen, should those multiple enterprises compete to supply the user? Or should their relationship be non-rival, with each enterprise having an entrenched position, such that cooperation among them must take place before the service in question can be provided? Table 4.3 summarizes the possible dimensions of choice for this aspect of service organization.

Sometimes, of course, there is no choice, as in genuine natural monopoly cases. But that does not apply to many public services. If we look around, we can often see different ways of organizing the same service in different countries (as

Table 4.3: Patterns of public service provision

| | | Relationship | |
		Rival	Non-rival
Number of units	*Many*	1. Colleges under voucher scheme or pupil payment	2. Community Chest welfare associations
	Few	3. Regulated-competition services (e.g. regulated airlines)	4. Military forces (within a country)

with vehicle roadworthiness testing, referred to in section I) or in the same country at different times (as with the introduction of limited competition into trunk telecommunications service in the USA and UK, with Japan edging in the same direction at the time of writing).

There are two quite contradictory approaches to this choice in academic administrative thought. The only thing that the two approaches have in common, as Niskanen (1975, p. 640) observes, is the belief that it can make a difference whether public services come from a single provider or from a plurality of providers and, if it is the latter, whether the relationship among those enterprises is one of rivalry or complementarity.

One tradition, based on military–bureaucratic ideas, sees competition as appropriate only for private services, and argues that public services should be supplied by monopolies. This might be argued on several grounds. One is that the 'public sector' should behave as a single actor. One enterprise should not be able to destroy or undo the work of another. That is what is being ridiculed in the epigraph to this chapter, and it figures in innumerable works of fact and fiction on the subject of large-scale organization. Studies of the build-up of disasters often reveal the development of a problem which has fallen between the crevices of different jurisdictions, such that no one has seen the complete picture (see Turner, 1974; 1978; Bennett, 1983).

Another possible argument against multiple providers is that public services often have 'customers' who are negatively rather than positively valued – down-and-outs, the mentally ill, the physically handicapped, the unemployed. Competition among suppliers for such services may well turn out to be negative – to avoid responsibility for awkward cases, rather than (or as well as) positively jockeying to serve favoured customers (Hood, 1976, pp. 18–19). Rivalry in such a case may not produce better service to the consumer, but 'Gresham's Law', with standards being driven down to the level of the worst provider. Putting services under a single roof or 'one-stop shop' run by a single provider, may sometimes offer a better prospect of service to 'unattractive' users than fragmentation of provision among a set of autonomous enterprises.

Third, competition in the provision of public services may be held to be wasteful of resources, in the same way as it is sometimes said that advertising rivalry between tobacco companies is wasteful, on the grounds that a few big firms dominate the market offering virtually the same product, and that costs and prices could be lower in the absence of advertising. The great exponent of this view was Edwin Chadwick, the famous English nineteenth-century radical. He advocated the replacement of simultaneous rival supply for services such as gas, water, railways and even funeral services by 'competition for the field' – that is, competitive periodic tendering for monopoly rights to operate such services. This combined, in his view, the advantages of single-provider organization with the advantages of competition and private ownership (Crain and Ekelund, 1976).

Fourth, when it comes to multiple but non-rival providers for a service, it may be argued on transactions cost grounds that a structure which requires agreement among many separate enterprises will be heavily (and perhaps undesirably) biased towards inertia. Pressman and Wildavsky (1973) argue this on the basis of a multiplicative combination of autonomous possibilities. If a project, to be carried out successfully, requires cooperation among a set of autonomous enterprises, each of which occupies a non-substitutable position, there is a potential for the familiar 'holdout' problem that we encountered in Chapter 1 (where a legal transaction requires the consent of many separate parties before it can be of any value, as in the case of the servitudes needed to lay the water pipes to V).

Pressman and Wildavsky's analysis, briefly, goes like this. Suppose that a project requires action by two separate enterprises A and B. Suppose further that there is a 0.95 probability that each enterprise will:

(a) be willing to take part in the joint project;
(b) participate competently; and
(c) carry out its part of the project quickly.

These assumptions are generous. Enthusiasm, competence and speed are taken to be very nearly, but not quite, certain. In some real-life cases I have known, a probability of 0.05 would be closer to the mark. Now, when two independent probabilities are put together they combine multiplicatively rather than additively, so that the joint probability of such a project being executed with enthusiasm, competence and speed is $0.95 \times 0.95 = 0.90$. This is still high, at 9 chances out of 10.

But, even if we hold to the generous assumption that there is 0.95 probability that each participant enterprise will act with enthusiasm, competence and speed, the *joint* probability of expeditious, etc. common action will steadily drop the more independent enterprises are involved. Once we get to 14 such enterprises, the joint probability of expeditious, etc. action drops below 0.5 – i.e. it is more likely that the joint project will fail than that it will succeed. If the probability of enthusiasm, competence and speed in the participation of each enterprise is set at a less generous level – say, at 0.75 (still high by many real-world standards) – it only takes three separate enterprises to reduce the joint probability of success below 0.5, and thus to make failure more likely than success.

This is a slightly different twist to the familiar holdout problem, and is used by Pressman and Wildavsky to highlight what they see as the negative side of providing public services through many independent but non-substitutable enterprises. However, their stark conclusions depend on assuming:

(a) that all participants are of exactly equal weight and importance in achieving the joint result;
(b) that the probabilities of each party playing its part enthusiastically, competently and speedily are quite

independent, in that there are no circumstances which
might jointly affect all of them; and

(c)   that each enterprise is absolutely non-supplantable and in
that sense has a headlock on the project as a whole, for
instance by a legal monopoly of some necessary kind of
authority.

Once differential weightings are introduced to reflect skewed
patterns of dominance and dependency and/or the
assumptions of completely independent probabilities and non-
substitutability of each participant are modified, the picture
alters significantly. Pressman and Wildavsky's rather dismal
conclusions become much less inevitable.

Such are the grounds on which it might be argued that poor
service will result from using multiple enterprises subject to
limited or no common direction. They are strongly entrenched
in traditional European theories of public administration.
They imply a very optimistic view about the controlability and
consumer-responsiveness of monopoly enterprises, and about
the fiduciary rather than opportunistic dispositions of those
who run such enterprises.

Completely counter to the traditional 'one service–one
enterprise' preference of traditional public administration
theory is the tradition of classical economics, with its
preference for competition as a way to limit slack in enterprises
and bring benefits to the consumer. This preference rests on a
pessimistic view of the controlability and consumer-
responsiveness of monopolies. Conventionally, competition is
assumed to wipe out enterprises operating other than at least
cost, and to force those which have not yet been wiped out to
seek new strategies (see Nelson and Winter, 1982). It does not
matter whether enterprises consciously aim for least costs or
maximum profits, or whether their strategies derive from rules
of thumb or historical accident. Competition will simply see to
the elimination of all enterprises other than those which
happen, for whatever reason, to be maximizing profits (Elster,
1983, p. 5). The potential benefits of competition are often
argued to apply in other fields, too. For instance, Adam Smith
argued that competition for litigants' court fees by rival law
courts resulted in speedier and more convenient service to

litigants (Rosenberg, 1960, p. 564). Faced with a choice between 'fragmentation' and monopoly, this school of thought will tend to opt for the former. For instance, Niskanen (in Weiss and Barton, 1980, p. 173) claims that 'competition among bureaus may reduce the probability that the expected task is accomplished, but it increases the probability that the right task wil be accomplished, often in unexpected ways'.

Of course, even the most dyed-in-the-wool advocate of competition will recognize that not all public services can be provided by multiple enterprises continually and simultaneously offering rival sources of supply. That certainly applies to the examples with which this book began – the river mouth works at M and the water-supply enterprise for V. Adam Smith himself, the great exponent of the 'hidden hand' benefits of competitive markets, actually favoured temporary local monopolies in cases where such an arrangement was the only way effectively to develop specialized enterprise (Smith, 1978, pp. 85–6).

But even if some degree of monopoly is unavoidable, there is more than one way in which it can be constituted. Chadwickian 'competition for the field' is still possible. So is league tabling. For example, Parks and Ostrom (1982), on the basis of study of US police services, argue that where a number of small local monopolies provide services of the same general kind in contiguous areas, it is much harder for the service producers to conceal information about demand, input prices, alternative activities and their consequences, than would be the case for large, incommensurate or non-contiguous monopolies. Indeed, they claim that US police agencies tend to be more efficient in metropolitan areas where there are a large number of other police agencies.

Moreover, even where any kind of rivalry in service supply is impracticable, a case may be put for a set of non-rival multiple enterprises rather than a single monopoly provider. It may be held that such a structure is more likely to lead to careful performance appraisal by involving formal contracts and terminable agreements, as must apply when legally separate enterprises work together.

Indeed, there are more overtly political arguments for a multiple enterprise structure. These echo the case for concurrent powers in a federal system of government, in which no one single actor exercises unlimited prerogatives. This case for public service provision by multiple autonomous units goes back at least as far as Montesquieu, but has vigorous present-day advocates, such as Ostrom (1974).

From this viewpoint, Pressman and Wildavsky's analysis is not seen as an unshakeable argument for monopoly provision of public services. On the contrary, this line of argument runs, the more autonomous enterprises there are, the more likely it is that bad policies will be stalled before take-off rather than crashing from a great height later. A multiple enterprise structure may subject the quality of policy assumptions to more stringent tests and require a broader basis of consent before action than a single enterprise one. Smooth implementation of a policy unilaterally decided upon by a single individual or group, is not the only desideratum to be met in designing public service organization. Concurrent powers systems have their advantages as well as their drawbacks.

A third possible case for providing public services through multiple enterprises has already been touched upon in section III. That is, multiple unit structures may enable us to have our cake and eat it in a way which would not be possible in single unit structure. We may be able to interweave different types of enterprise in combination and so to resolve some of the inescapable dilemmas that arise when constituting a single enterprise, given the potential conflicts in the other design criteria considered in this chapter. At a multi-enterprise level of organization, such contradictions do not need to be sharply resolved on the drawing-board. Each criterion can be embodied into an enterprise, such that (barring deadlock) the advantages of each can be recognized and that no single one is set in concrete – the balance among them being continually adjustable by bargaining and negotiation.

For instance, Montesquieu long ago claimed that a confederate republic was a structure which simultaneously offered the advantages of large and small scale organization (Ostrom, in Kaufmann, Ostrom and Majone, 1986, pp. 117–8). A lower-level example of the same sort is the arrangement whereby a number of social welfare charities combine into a community chest structure for fund-raising. This potentially combines the benefits of larger-scale organization in publicity and fund-raising with the benefits of smaller-scale organization in service provision.

VI. GENERAL FUND VERSUS SPECIAL FUND BUDGETING

Public services do not come free. How are they to be paid for? This is a vital choice in organizing such services. Consider three possible ways of financing a public service.

(1) The consumer pays for what he uses, as and when he uses it. The exactness with which payment relates to use may, of course, vary. Some bus services, for instance, charge a flat fare for each ride, regardless of distance. Others charge fares which increase with distance travelled. Some telephone companies meter and charge for local calls per unit. Others make no charge for local calls, covering the cost from rental and trunk call charges. Often, some users (children, the elderly, the unemployed) are exempt from charge, so that others have to pay more.

(2) Funds from a specific tax might go to pay for a particular service. There is no direct link between what each user pays and what he consumes, unlike pure per unit charges, but the source of funds for the service is clear. Such taxes might be payable by all users, as with road tolls, radio and TV licence fees. Or only some users might have to pay, as with British lighthouses, which are paid for by taxes on ships putting in to port. Indeed, such a tax might be levied only on non-users (say, an unemployment welfare tax on those in work). A variant is the compulsory insurance premium (perhaps with choice of insurer, as with health care services in many countries), which is hard to distinguish from tax-based provision if there is entitlement to unlimited service.

(3) The service might be paid for out of general fund taxes. That is, whoever provides service is periodically allocated a block of money for the job out of general tax revenue, as part of a general budgetary process. Unlike funding from special taxes, the tax cost of each particular service is not clearly visible

to the ordinary consumer. Before the French Revolution, general fund financing of public services was the exception rather than the rule. Today, of course, it is commonplace.

Any number of hybrids of these forms are possible. A large body of writing is devoted to detailed and technical discussion of such financing choices. Here, it is only possible to sketch out some of the ways in which different methods of paying for public services might shape the behaviour of opportunistic producers and consumers.

Economics-based 'public choice' analysis tends to highlight the potential drawbacks of general-fund budgeting – (3) above (see Mueller, 1979, pp. 90–6). That approach, the argument goes, is ripe for the exercise of producer-group opportunism, because budget negotiations usually involve small-numbers relationships. That means information-impactedness, since information needed to assess claims for funds will be largely in the hands of those who are making the claims. So budgeting turns into a political poker game between and among budget allocators and budget claimants.

Many economic theories of budgeting build on a variant of Niskanen's (1971) assumption that budget allocators are wholly ignorant of public service 'production functions' (that is, the costs of providing services in different ways). In such conditions, budgeting will be marked by: recurrent crises, largely created by the participants as bargaining tactics; protracted negotiations (all-night sittings, unshaven press conferences at dawn, etc.); frequent deadlocks; melodrama. The outcome of the process will certainly reflect bargaining skill, stamina and political muscle as well as (perhaps) an element of luck. It may or may not reflect what users or consumers of public services want.

Under such a system, service providers (be they contractors or public bureaucracies) will neither stand to gain from cutting costs nor to lose from failure to do so. Any such gains or losses will be shared among a mass of taxpayers. Worse, producers may tend to gain *fewer* resources from general tax funds, not more, if they find ways of providing service at lower costs. The opportunist is therefore motivated to think up new tasks or to push up the costs or quality of service, not to cut costs. And when pressed to trim budgets, opportunistic producers may choose to cut back disproportionately on their most visible or necessary services rather than to 'trim the fat' in other areas of activity (cut the funds for filling in pot-holes in the road but not for senior staff conferences in Hawaii), so as to build up a dramatic and visible picture of inadequate funds and to build up political support for more in the next budget round (see Hood and Wright, 1981, pp. 208–9).

Moreover, the argument runs, even if service producers do not act opportunistically in general fund budgeting, users may still do so. This problem is termed 'moral hazard'. Moral hazard arises when someone other than the immediate consumer pays part or all of the cost of what the consumer uses, as in the well-known case of medical care (Breyer, 1982, p. 33). Niskanen (1971, p. 143) likens the effect of general fund financing of public services to that of averaging the bill for a group of diners at a restaurant. Under such an arrangement, each diner – if he or she is opportunistic – has a clear incentive to order a higher-priced meal than he would do if the bills were paid individually. Restaurateurs, naturally, favour this approach too. Moreover, incentives for users to alter their consumption when costs change are weak. For instance, suppose that tougher anti-pollution rules raise the cost of electricity production. If power is paid for by user-charges, higher tariffs will put pressure on consumers to cut consumption. If electricity is paid for out of general taxes, there would be no incentive for the self-regarding user to cut consumption (tragedy of the commons again). The collective cost goes through the roof.

In such conditions, services financed from general tax funds must be rationed, such that there will be 'unmet needs' – for instance, by brown-outs or blackouts in a general tax-financed system of electricity supply. To avoid such rationing, provision must be at the level which would be demanded if those services really were free. As a rule, people want more of services which are free than of services for which they have to pay per unit of consumption. So to meet demand for 'free' services, more of them must be produced than the users would be willing to pay for, even if they were given the money cost of the amount demanded under moral hazard conditions and charged for their use at cost instead. If resources in general are scarce, that level of service provision must be paid for by forcing individuals collectively to consume less of other services which, in the absence of moral hazard, they would prefer. Hence, where their producers or consumers (or both) are opportunistic, service provision from general tax funds will unavoidably raise difficult questions about the real 'need' for each service. The public choice argument is that such questions will be easier to resolve by using charges or service-specific, earmarked taxes.

Such problems cannot be brushed aside. But special fund financing has its limits too.

First, user charges are infeasible for pure public goods.

Second, where the service involves natural monopoly (e.g. V's piped water supply), financing from charges will not necessarily keep slack under control. Regulations on charges, for instance, may run into information-impactedness on supply costs.

Third, other difficult issues may arise in fixing charges. Should one group of customers subsidize another group? Who is to pay the extra cost of new facilities needed to meet rising demand in increasing costs-to-scale services or to meet peaks of demand for variable demand services? The politics of user charges, as we noted in Chapter 1, tends to hinge on which users pay what charges.

Fourth, charges which are *precisely* proportioned to quality and quantity of use are typically costly to levy, in time and equipment. Even for private goods and services, such considerations often lead to the imposition of charges which are not directly related to use, as we saw earlier. Sometimes it costs more to collect charges than to allow resource to be used free. For instance, revenue from tolls for little-used car parks, bridges, roads, beaches, park benches, may be less than the cost of collecting the tolls, let alone that of maintaining the facilities.

Fifth, in cases where some services are paid for by taxes and other potentially substitutable services are financed by general tax funds, charges may distort patterns of use. For instance, if per unit charges are levied for solid waste collection, opportunistic consumers might try to get rid of as much garbage as possible through (general tax-financed) sewers, via trash-mashers, perhaps raising the tax costs of running the sewage system.

Sixth, where those on low incomes are exempt from charges (as often happens in practice with user charges), the moral hazard problem reappears. The practical reality of charge-based service provision is full of such problems (see Heald, 1983, pp. 299–306, for a fuller discussion).

Very similar issues arise in the fixing of special fund taxes. Such taxes (as with user-charges) will certainly make the cost of each individual service more visible to those who pay the taxes. Part of the usual case for paying for services in this way is that citizens must balance desires for better quality service against identifiable tax costs, whereas the costs of each service are more opaque under general fund financing. That is most likely to happen when earmarked taxes are highly visible and 'lumpy' – for instance, when the taxpayer must pay large sums at irregular intervals, rather than painlessly and automatically added as minor additions to retail prices. However, those kinds of taxes – as with dog licences, auto licences, radio and TV licences – tend to be difficult to enforce, for reasons discussed in Chapter 3. Moreover, earmarked tax provision does not necessarily avoid the moral hazard problem, since by definition tax payable is not proportioned to use. And the information-impactedness problem, especially for monopoly providers, may be just as severe in fixing specific tax rates as it is for allocating block grants from a general fund budget.

The drawbacks of general fund financing must therefore be set against the drawbacks of special fund taxes and user charges. It is naive to suppose that one or other form of financing is a panacea, although, as with many other dimensions of choice in public service organization, slogans such as 'charges good, taxes bad', and vice versa, tend to be advanced as universal prescriptions, without consideration of the specifics of the service involved or of what kind of charges or taxes might be applied (see Heald, 1983, p. 306).

VII. PRIVATE ENTERPRISE OR PUBLIC BUREAUCRACY

In the last chapter (section III), we looked at the issue of whether law enforcement should be done by private enterprise or public bureaucracy. The same choice arises in organizing any public service. A public bureaucracy, under political direction, might do the job, or the work might be done under contract or licence by a company, independent association or a similar institution. Would it make any difference? If so, how much difference would it make?

How much difference the choice of public bureaucracy versus private enterprise is likely to make will depend in part on how the other choices in service organization are handled. For instance, changing from a public bureau monopoly to a monopoly private enterprise contractor for garbage collection (as in many European cities) is likely to make less difference than (say) using public bureaucracy in some parts of a town and private enterprise in others, or using a voucher scheme to allow each household to choose its waste disposal contractor from an approved list, which might conceivably include public as well as private enterprise operators.

But public bureaucracy certainly has some features which usually differentiate it from private enterprise. By definition, public bureaucracy in its classic form involves (a) direct political direction of operations; and (b) public or community ownership.

The implications of political direction for law enforcement were discussed in the last chapter. We saw that political direction in that case can avoid some of the problems which would otherwise arise in framing rules precisely (so as to avoid over- or under-inclusiveness) and of proportioning enforcement effort negatively to the severity of punishments, to save on law enforcement costs. Day-to-day political direction shares the general advantages of direct employment over performance contracts, in that it cuts down the cognitive load on rule-making capacity and avoids the need to foresee and provide for all contingencies in advance.

It also shares some of the general drawbacks of the master–servant relationship. It tends to generate elaborate clearance rules for conducting business, with prudence dictating that potentially difficult issues be passed up to or towards the political directorate. It is often said that a prime 'bureaucratic imperative' is to stay out of political trouble and avoid risk (Mashaw, 1983, pp. 69, 74). Elected public officials will thus carry a heavy load of case-work, with delays as cases queue for decision. Change will be a political process, requiring the ability to convince those at the top that things need changing, whereas in a marketplace innovation may be prompted by the prospect of individually appropriable financial gains or losses.

Moreover, part of the case for direct political oversight, as we saw, is that 'wider issues' can be brought into play at any time. That means that any service provided through public bureaucracy is likely to become overlaid with purposes extraneous to that service. For instance, public contracts may be used to prop up ailing firms or to enforce price-control measures ('cross-sanctions' enforcement, as discussed in the last chapter) instead of simply performing a specific task at least cost. A case can certainly be made for flexible and multi-purpose enterprise of this kind in some conditions, as we have seen. But it inevitably means that the output or cost-effectiveness of any one such bureaucracy will tend to be intangible or hard to measure by any single yardstick. Non-politically sensitive issues will be hard to disentangle from politically sensitive ones. This gives scope for the exercise of opportunism by bureaucrats who wish to avoid work or stress.

The second basic defining feature of public bureaucracy is public ownership. Ownership of such enterprises is not transferable through bankruptcy or trading in stocks, so that gains or losses from their operations are unavoidably – and compulsorily – spread among the population at large. If bureaucrats are opportunistic, this gives little incentive for X-efficiency. Failure to limit slack is punished, if at all, only by an uncertain political process, not by a high probability of takeover or liquidation; and equally success in cutting costs is not rewarded in any direct material sense. Monitoring performance thus requires a heavy burden of evaluation or audit, through extensive and case-specific investigation. And that in turn demands elaborate and costly record-keeping so that such checks can be made.

This does not *necessarily* apply to private enterprise provision. Indeed, if private enterprises work in competitive capital markets, elaborate administrative procedures for controlling slack will not be needed, however opportunistic the people involved may be. Self-indulgent investment decisions will be penalized by the capital market in the form of discrimination in interest rates and successful investment decisions can be rewarded by appreciation in the value of stock options. Transferability of ownership will ensure that if the enterprise is run other than at the least-cost combination of inputs, its stock price will depreciate to the point where capital gains are realizable by other investors buying the stock at the depreciated price, taking over control of the enterprise and managing it at lower cost per unit of output – or, in the event of bankruptcy, breaking up the enterprise altogether and putting its assets to more productive uses in other hands (Wagner, 1973). Such processes may serve to limit slack even for an enterprise which is not operating in a competitive product market. To the extent that such circumstances prevail, the provision of public services through such enterprises will require no very elaborate checking and oversight procedures, and reporting, record-keeping and audit can be kept to a minimum.

This is, needless to say, an idealized picture. But it gives us a yardstick to use in the public bureaucracy/private enterprise choice. The case for using private or independent enterprise will be weak if it can be shown that in practice the factors which might in theory limit X-inefficiency in transferable-ownership enterprises (and which cannot *even* in theory operate to limit X-inefficiency in public bureaucracies), operate weakly or not at all. For instance, in the drive legally to 'privatize' what were formerly public bureaucracies in the UK in the recent years, substantial barriers have been erected to transferability of ownership in the 'privatized' enterprises, as well as to product-market competition. This goes sharply against the *raison d'être* of privatization.

The classic public bureaucracy potentially brings 'finger-tip' political control of operations at a cost of difficulty in limiting slack. Pure private enterprise provision of service potentially combines easier control of slack with less political responsiveness. So it is not surprising that many public services in practice are provided by 'hybrid' enterprises, which are neither classic public bureaucracies nor pure private enterprises.

Space does not allow detailed discussion of this phenomenon here. Such enterprises typically have their own legal personality, so that they are not under direct political oversight (thus limiting the need for elaborate and extensive clearance procedures), but often have the public bureaucracy feature of non-transferable ownership (with the consequent problem of fixing audit and reporting requirements to control slack). This is often done, for instance, to combine some possession of 'public power' (for which transferability of ownership is deemed unsuitable) with fairly straightforward service operations – such as combining trading activities with legal monopoly, regulatory powers, powers to raise taxes, or powers to acquire land compulsorily. The popularity of 'hybrid' enterprises of this kind suggests that they are often seen – perhaps illusorily – as a way of avoiding some of the potentially unpleasant side-effects associated with using either pure public bureaucracy or pure private enterprise in providing public services.

VIII. CONCLUSION

This chapter has reviewed some of the basic choices which have to be faced in organizing public services. Necessarily, that has meant skimming lightly over a vast terrain. Few subjects are as much written about as that of organization. In spite of that – or maybe because of it – 'organization' remains one of the fuzziest terms of administrative discourse.

In principle, before designing organization for public services, we should carefully consider each of these dimensions *separately*, in the specific circumstances of each case. Even on the six very simple dimensions of organization reviewed here, the number of possible configurations is very large. For instance, if each of the six dimensions is divided (very crudely) into only two types (as in Table 4.4), and if we suppose that the organization of any public service can be some combination of those 12 types, that gives 4095 possible types of organization to be considered. Subdivide those categories, as has been done even in the elementary discussion of each of them in the preceding sections, and the array of possible institutional choice takes a further quantum leap in complexity.

Table 4.4: Six dimensions of choice in public service organization and twelve extreme points

Dimension	Extreme points	
Specialization	1. A specialist for everything	2. Do-it-yourself service
Scale	3. The world	4. Immediate neighbourhood
Contract	5. Every task done through direct employment contracts	6. Every task done through specific performance contracts
Number of service providers	7. Only one source of supply	8. Large number of units or enterprises engaged in provision of service
Financial basis	9. Block grant from general tax fund only	10. Special fund finance from specific levies or user-charges only
Legal or constitutional type of providing enterprise(s)	11. Public bureaucracy only	12. Private or independent enterprise only

Organizing public services thus involves more than a simple choice between public and private. Perhaps because of the potential complexity of the choice, discussion of organization often concentrates on a small subset of the types of dimensions considered here. Take the well-known public choice approach to public service organization, which has been referred to at several points in this chapter. Many public choice analysts have emphasized the institutional shortcomings of a type of organization which occupies an extreme point on all six dimensions of organization considered above, representing a combination of all the left-hand characteristics on Table 4.4 – that is, specialized/large-scale/direct employment/single provider/general tax fund-financed/public bureaucracy. Indeed, such approaches often *define* public bureaucracy in terms of those positions on the other five characteristics.

Such polemics have certainly breathed some new life into the mouldering bones of administrative analysis. Much of traditional public administration thinking and teaching did tend to dwell on describing and/or justifying that style of organization, without much treatment of the alternatives. At the same time, stipulative definitions of public bureaucracy in such terms do beg a lot of questions. And certainly, to go bald-headedly to the *other* extreme on those six dimensions, in the sense of a combination of all the right-hand characteristics of Table 4.4 – i.e. do-it-yourself/micro-scale/performance contract-based/multi-enterprise/user-charge-financed/private enterprise provision – is unlikely to be any panacea either, for reasons discussed earlier. So the 4093 cases in the range between those two extreme configurations deserve some attention.

Of course, even 4095 possible options strains our capacity for rational choice, in the sense of the capability to work through all the possibilities to determine which configuration seems best in the circumstances of any particular service. Moreover, there is not much to go on in the way of reliable factual evidence about the consequences of adopting one institutional arrangement rather than another. (Limited space means that this chapter has had to concentrate on laying out standard lines of argument rather than describing empirical studies, so this point cannot be elaborated here.)

In practice, of course, many of the 'choices' considered here are made unthinkingly, by default or in a reflex way. Options are not systematically examined because choosers are conditioned to take some kinds of institutional arrangements as preferable to or more 'natural' than others. Analysis should be least help us to open these choices up, to identify the options and the questions to ask about those options, so that we can begin to recognize alternatives and argue about them coherently.

QUESTIONS FOR REVIEW

1. What would be the arguments for and against performing the flood-control works at V by (a) public bureaucracy, and (b) private or independent enterprise?

2. ˹ How would you want to organize the following public services and why?
   (a) The mowing of grass on village greens.
   (b) The provision of satellite facilities for assisting undersea rescue work in the Pacific Ocean.
   (c) The control of extortion gangs in big cities.

3. Suppose that a report has highlighted some overlap and duplication in the public services offered by the Ministry of Almost Everything and the Ministry of Everything Else. Accordingly, the report proposes to merge the two ministries into a single, comprehensive Ministry of Everything, in order to increase efficiency and to prevent division of responsibility for the services involved. What questions would you want to ask in evaluating such a proposal?

4. At the time of writing, policemen are estimated to commit more than one-third of all crimes in Mexico City. What are the options which might be considered as means for reducing this particular manifestation of the 'servant problem'?

GUIDE TO FURTHER READING

The literature on organization is, as has been indicated, inexhaustible. Perrow (1979) offers a good sociology-based introduction to this topic, though he focuses – as do most sociology-based approaches – on 'organizations', in the sense of corporate enterprises or plants within them, rather than organization in the broader sense used in this chapter. Well-known economics-based approaches to the analysis of organization at the enterprise level include Niskanen (1971);

Williamson (1975); Liebenstein (1976); Jackson (1982); Parks and Ostrom (1982).

For the provision of public services through multi-enterprise structures – sometimes referred to in economics language as public service 'industries' – well-known explorations include Ostrom, Tiebout and Warren (1961); Ostrom and Ostrom (1965); Ostrom, Parks and Whitaker (1978). Sociology-based explorations of the same issue include Hanf and Scharpf (1978), pp. 345–70; and Hjern and Porter (1981), pp. 211–27.

For attacks on the traditional or dominant theories and doctrines of public administration, see Ostrom (1974) and Sharpe (1986). For examples of studies explicitly directed to the question of the relation between organization structure and performance in the provision of public services, see Savas (1977) and Ostrom, Parks and Whitaker (1977).

5 Handling Change: Adaptation

'Everything that happens is grossly improbable . . .' (Beer, 1966, p. 55)

I. THE ADAPTATION PROBLEM

Organizing public services and making and enforcing rules would be difficult enough even in a Shangri-La world where nothing ever changed. But the need to adapt to change lies at the heart of many of the issues which have been reviewed in the last three chapters. It is the Achilles' heel of the 'rules not men' approach to rule-making and of the machine approach to enforcement, as we saw. The problem of how to organize public services can never be solved once and for all, if only because the context in which public services are operated rarely remains static for long. Circumstances of one kind or another conspire to make the rules out-of-date, to throw the enforcement machinery out of gear, to destroy the foundations on which service organization is built. So this chapter brings the adaptation problem into the centre of the stage and gives it some separate attention.

Consider the following nine hypothetical cases:

(1) Solid waste from individual homes in a town (T) has traditionally been disposed of by a mixture of dumping at landfill sites and combustion in incinerator plants. Use of electronic gadgets of all kinds in T is sharply rising, and so domestic garbage comes to contain an ever-larger quantity of spent batteries from such gadgets. Given the traditional methods of waste disposal, this is a problem, because the silver batteries used for watches and other electronic devices contain a high concentration of mercury. That means atmospheric

pollution if the batteries are incinerated or dangerous seepage into the soil if they are dumped at landfill sites . . .

(2) Car parking in the downtown area of a developing city (C) becomes a major problem, with an acute shortage of parking lots and streets severely obstructed by parked vehicles, hampering emergency services. The city authorities respond to the problem by enacting a rule that all new commercial buildings in the downtown area must include facilities for off-street parking by all employees and visitors. Ten years later, C's downtown parking problem is completely solved, but traffic congestion now brings the city to a complete standstill, with every worker trying to commute by car . . .

(3) In the case of V, as described in Chapter 1, a freak storm of unprecedented severity suddenly breaches the natural sea-wall (B). Quite unexpectedly, V is now wide open to a threat of serious coastal flooding from which it was previously protected. Spring tides are approaching and strong onshore gales are forecast . . .

(4) A and B are towns fairly near to one another. A's population is rising fast, creating a massive build-up in demand for water, power and road facilities and causing acute drainage problems on its low-lying land. B on the other hand, is suffering a sudden drop in its population, leaving it with a huge surplus of redundant, high-quality public utility facilities and a reduced tax base from which to maintain those facilities . . .

(5) The movie *Stilt-wheels* has taken the youth of a country (D) by storm. Suddenly pavements and parks everywhere are full of teenagers roller-skating in pairs on three huge stilts (the nearer legs of the pair being strapped together, as in a three-legged race) following the pattern used in the movie. National competitions are organized, and there is even talk of a stilt-wheel Olympics. When charged that the cult is dangerous both to its practitioners and third parties, youthful stilt-wheel enthusiasts complain of the complete lack of special facilities for the safe practice of the sport in D, in contrast to more established forms of recreation . . .

(6) Since records began about 150 years ago, the lowest temperature registered in the city E was 5 degrees Celsius. Accordingly, the water pipes of the city are laid only just below the ground, making them very cheap to instal and repair. For a

few days, E is suddenly gripped in a polar airstream, with temperatures between $-1°$ and $-10°$. All main water pipes freeze solid, and for the few days that this persists, water consumers are put to extreme inconvenience . . .

(7) Weather modification technology develops to the point where weather conditions need no longer be taken as given. Massive new incompatible-use problems result. For instance, X wants to engineer a dry weekend for promoting his pop festival, while in the same area Y wants to engineer a wet weekend for watering his barley crop (see Schmid, in Samuels and Schmid, 1981, p. 80). Conflict-of-use problems are getting beyond a joke . . .

(8) Satellite technology becomes available as a feasible means of surveillance over the behaviour of rivers and coastlines, using automatic monitors. Manual methods of doing the job suddenly appear obsolete . . .

(9) A public library instals automatic detectors at its exit door, using a radio or electromagnetic beam to identify tagged books being illicitly removed, as an alternative to uncertain and intrusive personal searches by a human security guard. After a few months, the detector ceases to pick up any cases of attempted book theft, and the library authorities congratulate themselves on getting the compliance rate up to 100 per cent (see section II, Chapter 3). However, a book check shows that books are disappearing just as fast as before the new detectors were installed. Investigations reveal that opportunistic evaders have taken to wearing clothes lined with a metallic element which acts as a shield against the detectors' beam . . .

How can public service arrangements come to terms with changes like these?

(1) Sources of Change in Public Service Provision

The nine cases given above show up at least five dimensions of change which can impinge on the provision of public services. Changes can differ in terms of their source and the way that they build up. They can also differ in terms of whether they are reactive or autonomous, whether they make or destroy public goods, whether they affect production or consumption of public services.

(a) *Variation in Source.* The changes which are causing problems in the nine cases above do not all spring from the same source. Some of the examples (cases (3) and (6)) come from changes in the biosphere, that is, the physical or natural world. Some of them (cases (1), (7), (8), (9)) come from changes in the technosphere, that is, the stock of human skills and knowledge in so far as it determines what we can produce and consume. Some of them (cases (2), (4) and (5)) come from changes in the sociosphere, that is, the way that human communities behave. Even if we could eliminate or damp down some of these sources of change, the others would still be there.

(b) *Variation in Build-up.* The nine cases differ in the way that change builds up. Many of them are developments which occur over a period rather than all at once. For instance, the battery disposal problem (1), the traffic congestion problem (2), the population change problem (4), even the weather modification problem (7), and the tritium-lined clothing problem (9), are likely to emerge cumulatively, although they may suddenly reach such proportions as to cause a crisis. Other changes come suddenly, all at once, without any warning, as with (3), (6), perhaps (5). (3) is a potentially lethal discontinuity in the assumptions on which the management of V has been built.

(c) *Variation in Autonomy.* The cases differ in the extent to which the changes involved are autonomous – that is, causally independent of the way that public services are provided. Most of the examples are developments that 'just happen', either through the uncertain wiles of nature ((3), (6)) or through the more or less autonomous development of technology or fashions ((1), (5), (7)). They are not reactions to the way that public services are provided. But (2) is *not* autonomous. It is an unforeseen result of the rules which govern downtown development in C. The population shift case (4) might well be the same, if it is caused in some measure by the public service package provided in the two towns (for instance, good services and/or low taxes in A, poor services and/or high taxes in B). Case (9) is a change which is totally reactive to the enforcement strategy used by the library authorities.

(d) *Creation or Destruction of Public Good or Joint Consumption Characteristics.* Some changes create public goods (as with the advent of modern explosives creating the possibility of controlling M, in the case of V). Other changes turn public or joint-consumption goods into individually consumable ones. In this way, new technical developments continually upset the assumption on which we found choices about public service organization. Case (7) is an example of a new technologically-created public good (people who don't pay for good weather can't be excluded, one person's enjoyment doesn't diminish another's, etc.). Broadcasting 60 years ago is a similar case of a newly created public good. Opportunistic listeners or viewers could tune into broadcast programmes without paying, unless compelled to do so. There is a 'tragedy of the commons' potential in radio broadcasting, too. Without rules limiting access, anyone could transmit at any time on any frequency, such that the 'common' (the radio spectrum) becomes worthless, albeit temporarily (Minasian, 1969, pp. 391–403). A more modern example of the same kind is the way that space travel and satellite technology create a familiar public bad or nuisance problem in a new context, with the growth of 'junkyards in space'. A build-up of disused satellites, burnt-out rocket engines and other man-made debris potentially creates orbital congestion and makes for radio interference problems in communications between space and earth.

Equally, other technical changes serve to 'privatize' what were once public goods, or (which is perhaps more common) to create new varieties of public goods at the same time as destroying old ones. Cable TV transmission, for instance, produces only to a very limited extent the radio interference pollution problem involved in broadcasting over the airwaves, and also creates the possibility of charges proportionate to degree of use and of exclusion of those who do not pay for the service. It thus avoids the 'free rider' problem inherent in traditional broadcasting. But at the same time the laying of local cable networks creates natural monopoly and holdout problems in the negotiation of servitudes, as in the case of the piped water-supply to V. The development of technology for launching larger communication satellites is another potentially 'privatizing' force in broadcasting, since it means that satellites in space can now incorporate functions that once had to be handled in large ground stations (with potential natural monopoly effects), miniaturizing ground stations so that they will fit on to the top of a house like a TV aerial (Naisbitt, 1982, p. 12). The same technology applied to maritime information services is capable of cutting out the 'free rider' problem traditionally associated with the lighthouse approach to providing vessels with navigational information, potentially destroying what used to be a stock example of a public good.

(e) *Changes Affecting Production and Changes Affecting Consumption.* Some changes mainly affect 'consumption' of public services, others mainly affect production. Most of the nine cases above affect the pattern of consumption or demand for public services – rise and fall in overall demand (4), demands for new kinds of services (5) or for old services to be adapted to new needs (1), and so on. But (8) is a development which changes production possibilities for public services (it is, in fact, what eventually happened to the management of the River Nile, which for thousands of years was monitored in the same way, checking the water level against notched stone pillars built on the river banks by the Pharaohs). So is (9). (7), too, has obvious potential implications for the production of public services, for instance in flood control and water supply.

Of course, some changes affect supply and demand simultaneously. This will happen by definition where users also help to 'produce' public services to some degree, as in the case of do-it-yourself organization of public services (see section II of the last chapter). For instance, if users of garbage collection services become less disciplined in separating out different types of garbage for collection, in putting rubbish in the required places or otherwise using garbage-collection facilities as intended (for instance, by choking rubbish chutes in apartment buildings by putting large or bulky items down them), the garbage collection service will inevitably either deteriorate in quality or rise sharply in cost; or both. The point applies wherever some element of 'co-production' is involved in public service provision (see Hood, 1983, pp. 166–7).

In Chapter 3, we saw that changes in the 'technosphere' can affect methods of enforcing rules, by creating the possibility of new 'enforcement machines'. This applies especially in the sphere of surveillance or detection, sometimes in physical apprehensions too (as with automated carparks). But technical changes may also *undermine* the efficacy of enforcement machines, as in the case of (9). More generally, technical and other changes both destroy and create the properties which were associated with 'enforceability' in Chapter 3, section IV. It will be recalled that these factors were cadasterability, conduitability, standard-unequivocality, reinforceability and cross-sanctions. These factors may alter with changes in technology, so that administrative enforcement niches open and close.

For instance, radio receivers in the 1920s were fairly easily cadasterable. The equipment was large, fixed and required elaborate outside aerials for good reception. Such conditions made a fixed radio licence tax feasible as a way of paying for public service broadcasting (with its associated public good properties) in countries like Britain and the Netherlands in the 1920s. But after World War II, the developing portability and miniaturization of all radio sets eroded the cadasterability of the tax base, so that licence taxes for radio sets as such were abandoned in Britain in 1970 (Hood, 1985, p. 25), and tend to be administratively problematic in countries where they survive today, such as Malaysia and Singapore.

(2) Basic Requirements of Adaptivity

Nothing is for ever – not even the Pharaohs' system of managing the Nile. Somehow, changes such as the nine examples above must be coped with, provided for, adapted to, in the provision of public services. What exactly does it take to be adaptive?

Very generally, adaptation can be defined as the ability to spot material changes in circumstances, and the capacity and disposition to respond appropriately to those changes. Let us take that sentence to pieces again.

(a) *Capacity to Recognize Change.* Many horror stories about lack of adaptation in public service provision tell of failures to recognize the existence of changes in demand or of failure to take up new possibilities of production. Well-known examples include the survival of horse cavalry until the 1950s in the USA (Katzenbach, 1958) or the survival of quill-pen bureaucracy in the UK income tax structure for over two decades after the coming into existence of well-understood methods of automating routine tax administration (Hood, 1985, p. 16). Instruments designed to fight yesterday's wars are often, ironically, brought to a peak of excellence just as the problem to which they are addressed disappears. For example, ship registry and regulation in the UK is built in part on an apparatus designed to promote mercantilist economics and to protect Irish emigrants against epidemic disease during a 12-week sailing ship voyage from the British Isles to North America. The first element was begun in the Middle Ages and finally, with much administrative labour, brought to perfection just before mercantilism went out of favour in the nineteenth century. The second element was another baroque structure of rules to which the finishing touches were added just as the advent of steamships and the end of the Irish potato famine largely removed the original problem (MacDonagh, 1961).

(b) *Capacity to Respond.* One may have a very clear diagnosis of changes that are occurring, and yet have no power to do anything about it, making adaptation impossible. What is required is some stock or repertoire of alternative routines or the ability in some way to introduce variations into behaviour or structure.

(c) *Disposition to Respond.* One might have a clear perception of change, and the capacity to respond to it, but yet have no desire or motivation to do so. Deutsch (1983, p. 111) once defined political power as 'the ability to afford not to learn'. What is required is some source of selective pressure which rewards or reinforces appropriate responses and punishes failure to respond or inappropriate responses.

(d) *Appropriate Response.* 'Appropriateness' is obviously impossible to define in any scientific way, and often can be judged only with hindsight. But it is equally impossible to escape from the fact that some responses to change are appropriate and others are not, and the term adaptation is often reserved for the former. The standard example is the British Parliament's first response to the advent of the automobile, which was to limit its speed to 4 miles per hour (6.8 km/p.h.) and to require that it be preceded by a man on foot waving a red flag (Macrae, 1984, p. 89). This was certainly a 'response' to a new technological development, but we can now clearly see that it was appropriate, if at all, only as a short-term measure. In case (4) above, A might respond to its population surge simply by rationing out the existing services – say, by long daily power brown-outs or blackouts and daily shut-offs of the over-stretched water supply. B might respond to its population decline by taxing its few remaining citizens to the hilt to keep up the existing service capacity. Both are 'responses' to the change, in that *something* has been done about it. Whether they are *appropriate* responses, however, depends on circumstances. They might well be appropriate if A's population gain and B's population loss was very temporary – say, if A were suddenly swamped by a horde of incomers drawn to a faith-healer or if B suddenly lost population as a result of seasonal migration patterns or a loss of manpower due to a temporary war emergency. They would be entirely inappropriate if the population changes were permanent.

The next two sections look at the problem of spotting changes and of capacity to respond.

II. CAPACITY TO IDENTIFY CHANGES

Adaptation is impossible without some capacity to register and recognize change while there is still time to do something about it. In case (3), for instance, if the sea-wall B is breached at 2 a.m. on a dark night when everyone in V is asleep, and high tide is at 5 a.m., the whole place could suddenly be engulfed, Pompeii-style. But if someone is awake and gives the alarm, the village could be evacuated in the three hours available.

Of course, failure to register any change at all is an extreme case. Failure to appreciate the type and speed of change may be critical, too. For instance, it is well known that adaptive systems which work well enough within some range of variation in the environment may be overwhelmed by lethal discontinuities coming outside that range. Take the case of a cat sleeping in front of a fire. Even in its sleep, the cat moves nearer or further away from the fire so as to maintain a comfortable temperature on its skin. This is a standard example of what is conventionally termed 'homeostatic' control. The state of some system is automatically kept within a critical range without any elaborate cogitation, foresight, or high conscious understanding of the environment. What defeats adaptive systems of that kind is the sudden lethal discontinuity which goes outside the range of variation with which the system is programmed to cope – for instance, if the fire warming the sleeping cat suddenly turns into an explosion or a flood, as it might do if such a fire were burning on a sinking ship. To survive lethal discontinuities, it often takes cerebration, analysis, high consciousness, of a kind that is usually enormously expensive in resources and most of the time redundant in the performance of routine services (see Beer, 1966, p. 256; Steinbruner, 1974).

Morever, adaptation is commonly hampered or prevented:
(a) by failure to distinguish material changes from ephemeral or random disturbances;
(b) by failure to identify the turning point in a cycle;
(c) by failure to recognize the speed at which change is occurring;
(d) by failure to allow for reactive or strategic change.
Such problems are self explanatory and familiar enough, and so will only be briefly commented on.

(1) Distinguishing Material and Non-material Change
Survival as a stock market investor requires that you can distinguish a sudden 'hiccup' in the market from a movement presaging a significant slide or climb. Survival as a mountaineer requires that you can distinguish a few falling stones from the beginning of a landslide. Exactly the same problem presents itself in public service provision. Successful detection of enemy attacks requires an early warning system

that can distinguish a flock of geese from hostile missiles (as the North American system has in the past failed to do; see Bennett, 1983, p. 25).

Coming back to the nine cases considered earlier: does the sudden drop in E's temperature (case (6)) herald a shift to more extreme climatic conditions, such that the water authorities should now bury their pipes twice as deep, at huge expense? Or is it merely one of those once in a century climatic freaks? Is the stilt-wheeling explosion (case (5)) just another of those nine days' wonder movie cults that will quickly disappear without trace? Or is it the birth of a sport that has come to stay, as with the day that William Webb Ellis picked up a soccer ball and invented rugby football?

Where public service institutions are non-profit-making and adaptation is costly and effortful, there will often tend to be some inertia bias – a requirement to be convinced that a change is not a 'freak' before shaking everything up in response to it. To rush to provide large-scale stilt-wheeling facilities in case (5), for instance, would be to risk repeating the experience of those city authorities which responded to the 1970s skateboarding craze by planning skate parks, only to find that the craze was fizzling out just as the special parks were being finished. But equally, too strong an inertia bias runs the risk of dismissing an epoch-making change as a fad that will never catch on. The historical record is full of confident misjudgements of this kind. For instance, as late as 1910 the British Secretary of State for War went on record to state, 'we do not consider that aeroplanes will be of any possible use for war purposes'; and as late as 1930 it was generally thought that aeroplanes would never be suitable for trans-continental transport (these cases are noted by Jewkes *et al.*, 1969, p. 174).

(2) Spotting the Turning-Point

Closely related to the problem of distinguishing the 'nine days' wonder' from the permanent change is the problem of distinguishing a cycle from a trend, and then spotting the turning point in that cycle. This again is the classic problem of the stock market investor. Knowing that 'what goes up must come down' (or vice versa) isn't worth much. Everything hinges on the ability to spot turning-points. This problem can be serious in public service provision. Take the provision of services such as snow clearing or road gritting, to deal with the cycle of severe winter weather. In the Scandinavian countries, the snows, having once come, can usually be relied upon to lie for three months or so. In Britain, a little further south, spells of severe wintry weather can suddenly descend at any time over a five-month period, and once having come, often disappear again quite quickly, meaning that the change-identification aspect of adapting public services to winter weather conditions is inherently much more difficult in Britain than in Scandinavia.

A similar problem presents itself in some of the nine cases given in section I. In case (4), will A's population continue to grow towards mega-city proportions? Will B's population go on falling until B becomes no more than a hamlet? Or will their populations stabilize at some point? If so, where? In the case of (5), even if the craze is supposed to be temporary, how long will it last? Weeks, months, a year, a decade? In many cases, we cannot even be sure that the new problems we face are cycles or permanent changes, let alone spot the turning-points.

(3) Recognizing the Speed of Change
A third problem, even with permanent, uni-directional changes, is that of gauging the speed at which change is occurring. It is always dangerous to estimate speed of future change by looking at past trends. Suppose that in case (1) the garbage enterprise goes to the trouble and expense of building special plants for handling batteries, on a scale which assumes that use of batteries will go on rising at the rate of the recent past. Obviously, it will be left with unused capacity and wasted investment if, as it quite likely, the rate of increase levels off (perhaps as a result of saturation of the electronic-gadgets market or of the development of longer-life batteries). Undershooting and overshooting in scale of provision are pervasive in public service provision. The city authorities of B in case (4) might recognize and prepare for a downward drift in its population size, only to be completely bowled over by failing to anticipate the speed of the change, as with those US 'rustbelt' cities which lost nearly a quarter of their population during the 1970s.

(4) Allowing for Reactive Change
Often, the hardest change to anticipate is that which springs
from strategic response or reaction. The stock market investor
must gauge this, too. The success of his investment may depend
on his anticipation of other investors' actions, which in turn
may be based on an anticipation of his actions, and so on. The
same applies to many kinds of public service provision. In case
(9), those who devised the library security system did not
foresee how opportunists would respond to that system. In
case (2), those who framed the parking provision rule did not
anticipate how that rule would shape commuting choices by
downtown workers in C.

Anticipating the way in which consumers or users will
respond to new services, or new ways of providing old services,
can never be reduced to a technical formula, especially where
opportunism comes in. The building of roads, bridges, flood-
control works, may have an unexpected impact on the
distribution and intensity of human settlement. In the case of
V, works to stabilize M, if they are successful, may have a long-
term effect of raising real-estate prices and attracting incomers
to what has become a less hazardous place to live. Provision of
piped water supply will tend to increase household use of
water, once water is available at the turn of a tap rather than by
more laborious alternatives, such as fetching a bucket or
working a pump.

Hence, failure to adapt properly often springs from failure to
take account of reactive change, as opposed to extrapolating a
straight-line trend. One well-known way in which reactive
change can work is the so-called 'law of anticipated reactions'.
This says that production and consumption will change in
response to widely believed future disasters, shortages or gluts
of particular items, such that the forecasts which prophesied
the coming disasters etc., automatically become self-defeat-
ing, even though adaptation would be impossible without
those forecasts. For instance, in case (1), the citizens of
T may become so frightened by scares of mercury poisoning from spent batteries that their passion for battery-
powered electronic gadgets abates, causing them to return
to wind-up watches and the like, or to switch to rechargeable
batteries or mains-powered electronic gadgets, such that the

problem turns out to be less serious than was expected.

Another type of reactive change is what are sometimes termed 'regulation-response' sequences. For instance, as police acquire new technology (radio, radar speed-check equipment) opportunistic law-breakers obtain matching technology. Case (9) is, of course, a pure case of this. Regulation-response sequences do not only consist of technological innovation and counter-innovation, however. Reactive change often occurs within existing technology. For instance, as government debases the value of coinage, certain types of coins disappear as it becomes more profitable to melt them down for their metal value, until government in turn alters the metal content to correspond with their face value. As we saw in Chapter 2, the categories built into formal rules often set up incentives for opportunists to operate on the margins between one category and another. My Victorian forbears for a time made a living from building 99-ton sailing ships, since British government manning regulations of that time became more stringent for foreign-going vessels of 100 tons and above. With hindsight, such reactive responses to rules and enforcement strategies often seem inevitable, but they are often not anticipated at the time that the rules are framed or the enforcement strategy put into effect.

Correct identification of changes is thus a taxing condition to be met as a precondition for successful adaptation. Obviously, on top of the purely cognitive and intellectual problems in meeting that condition must be added all the emotional or political difficulties of facing up to change or displacing fixed beliefs (see Beer, 1966, p. 60). For instance, in the case of city B in example (4), we can well imagine difficulty in coming to terms with population decline as a result of wounded civic pride, reluctance to admit that the population loss is permanent or to tear down carefully planned and maintained facilities which provide employment, and so on. We can likewise imagine that the employees displaced by the new satellite technology in case (8) are unlikely to view that development with a completely open mind.

But failure to meet these conditions of change identification can be expensive. The downside risk of not recognizing change obviously varies. It may consist of operating services that are poorer and more expensive than they need to be, as in cases (4) or (9). It may amount to inconvenience and annoyance, as with the traffic snarl-ups in (2), the interruption of water supply in (6), the hazards to pedestrians in (5). Or it may mean serious loss of life or injuries, as with the mercury poisoning problem in (1) or the sea-wall collapse in (3).

As we saw in the last chapter (section III), the larger the scale of service provision, the greater the downside risk of change-detection errors is likely to be. In case (5), if some cities respond to the demand for stilt-wheeling facilities on the assumption that the sport has come to stay, while others make no response on the assumption that it is only a nine days' wonder, the consequence of working on whichever assumption turns out to be the wrong one will be less serious than if there had been a uniform national-scale response based on assumptions that turned out to be wrong.

III. CAPACITY TO RESPOND

As we saw in section I, changes in the biosphere, technosphere or sociosphere have a powerful potential for upsetting the assumptions on which public service provision are based. As we saw in section II, somehow registering or diagnosing material changes in supply or demand conditions is a precondition for successful adaptation – often a testing one.

But adaptation requires more than being able to register or diagnose change. A second condition is the capacity to vary behaviour or structure in some way in response to change – a means of providing 'mutants', in the language of biological evolution. There has to be a stock of ideas, a repertoire of routines, a set of instruments available, and some way of changing from the existing state of the system to a different one.

So this section discusses four common ways in which public service provision can be varied, in order to accommodate new purposes or circumstances. The four types overlap in practice and are intended only as a way of laying out the discussion.

Suppose that you have diagnosed a change in supply or demand conditions for a public service, as in the nine cases given in section I. Leaving aside the inertia response (do nothing, act as if no change were occurring), what might you do about it? You might:

(a) Slightly modify existing behaviour; that is, progressively differentiate and vary an established basic design.

(b) Recombine a set of existing but hitherto unrelated routines to serve a new purpose.

(c) Copy what others are doing; that is, imitate design features in use elsewhere.

(d) Work out a completely new design from scratch on your own; that is, develop a prototype without any significant copying or modification to an existing system.

(1) Piecemeal Adjustment: Differentiation and Variation of an Established Design

Perhaps the simplest way to change behaviour is to vary slightly an established procedure or design. For instance, when a new type of disease appears (AIDS, Legionnaires' disease, etc.), the first response of public authorities often consists of a slight modification of the existing public health rules to accommodate the new development – for instance, in requirements for compulsory notification, quarantine, and the like. Such an approach makes minimal demands on administration imagination and engineering capacity. It also limits risk, since if the design modification turns out to be a fiasco, steps can be retraced along a known path to get back to base. It builds on what is known to be workable. It makes possible the overhaul of rules and procedures with limited disruption to their day-to-day operation. And yet, pursued cumulatively, this approach can effect radical modifications to an original design.

Aversion to risk and desire for administrative practicality, as summed up in the familiar maxim 'start from where you are', often argue for this style of innovation. So it is not surprising to find that the story of many kinds of administrative adaptation can be told in these terms, as a cumulative, step-by-step differentiation and variation of what had existed before.

Indeed, this way of changing behaviour sometimes has positive advantages over more 'radical' ones. This applies for instance, when rules are being enforced on opportunistic evaders, since tactics can always be altered or reversed at a later stage of the game. In case (9), the library might hold its own against opportunistic book thieves rather better if it slightly modified its exit checking system at random intervals from time to time, rather than trying to solve the enforcement problem once and for all by a wonder machine. Tax administration almost everywhere uses piecemeal adjustment as a response to opportunistic evaders, for instance in the continuous modifications made to the tax treatment of the business executive's company-provided lunch, car, box at the opera, etc. Another case is the slow evolution of the ship registry rules in order to counter opportunistic evasion – for instance, in adding registration numbers to registered names to increase cadasterability; in introducing the additional requirement that each registered name should be unique and that registration numbers be carved into 'main timbers' to increase conduitability; and so on (see Jarvis, 1973, pp. 151–67).

This approach often involves resort to legal fiction and its administrative equivalents, as a way of treating a new situation as if it fell into the category of the old without changing the basic rules. This means adopting expedient but consciously false factual assumptions. For instance, the breach of the sea-wall in case (3) might fictionally be taken to be a breach of the banks of the river R as a means of empowering a flood tax commission whose scope rule restricted it to dealing with R, to tackle the new sea-wall problem. The weather modification problem (case (7)) might be tackled by treating modification of the weather as air pollution, so as to fit it into an existing set of rules.

Fuller (1967, p. 68) argues that fictions tend to accompany adaptations in the law, where new doctrines must be created to tackle new social and business practices. He gives the example (ibid., 69) of the development of the doctrine of vicarious liability for delicts or torts through fictions such as holding a master to be negligent for having hired a careless servant or maintaining that the master 'impliedly commands' whatever the servant does on his behalf – assumptions that are patently false as statements of fact.

Such adaptation is 'conservative' in that it accommodates change within the language and ideas of the existing rules. It is the facts that are bent to fit the rules rather than vice versa, thus creating minimal disruption to the conceptual fabric built into the rules. Fuller sees fictions in law as reflecting human intellectual adaptation more generally, especially in areas where there is commitment to conceptual comprehensiveness; that is, in circumstances where hard cases cannot simply be ignored on the grounds that they do not conveniently fit into a framework of ideas. The fantastic conceits of lawyers and even physicists in constructing fictions such as Maxwell's Demon (that famous but imaginary entity which can 'see' each individual atom and discriminate among them) spring from trying to grapple with the world in a comprehensive way. The same often applies to the provision of public services. For the garbage collection authorities in case (1) simply to ignore the spent battery problem as something that just doesn't fit in to the previously exhaustive categorization of rubbish as either dumpable or burnable would be like a judge leaving a weather modification case undecided because he had no opinion on the matter, or because there were no clearly formulated legal rules in that field.

Piecemeal adjustment, in fact, has considerable potential advantages as an adaptive response. It enables administrative design to be modified cheaply, simply and without deep cognitive understanding of disturbances in the administrative environment. As we have seen, such an approach has positive advantages in the context of reactive changes springing from opportunism, as in the ship registry story. To have a grand strategy and make a large 'once-for-all' move in such conditions may well be counter-productive.

Equally, the limitations of this approach are obvious enough. It may not offer an adequate response to sudden lethal discontinuities such as cases (3) and (7). As with the case of cat sleeping by the fire, mentioned in section II, simple non-analytic adaptive systems can be completely defeated by such discontinuities. Piecemeal adjustment, for instance, may not help much when we are trying to cope with major 'technology backfires', which are an inevitable concomitant of modern technological development. An example is sudden major telephone cable failure in a modern advanced city, such as happened in Tokyo in 1984. All at once, the communications system on which emergency services (fire, police, ambulance) ordinarily depend is completely destroyed; the on-line computer networks which connect branches of public service organization to a collective stock of information are totally blacked out. More than a slight modification of existing practices may be needed to keep services going in such conditions.

(2) Recombination

What is here called recombination incorporates piecemeal adjustment, but involves slightly more engineering sophistication. Recombination denotes the making of minor modifications *to each of a set* of well-established elements, rules, routines or operations, so that, when added together, a completely different effect is produced or a quite different purpose served. For instance, in the case of town B in case (4), institutions previously designed to handle population expansion (say, in re-zoning agricultural land for residential building, in planning expansion of public utility services, etc.) might all be reprogrammed to operate in reverse, so that a quite different total effect is produced.

Biological evolution relies heavily on the reshuffling of genes in reproduction to introduce variety into natural systems, and something similar can sometimes be done deliberately to artificial systems. For example, a minor reprogramming of the operations of each of the several robots on an automobile assembly-line, when added together, may result in a product quite different from the old one (say, a switch from producing cars to producing tanks). High-volume, 'mass-production' administrative bureaucracies which operate on a quasi-assembly-line basis – with tasks broken down into tiny fragments of 'robotized' routines – can often be 'reprogrammed' in an analogous way. Tax bureaucracies, for instance, can be programmed to give money to people instead of taking it away from them, to collect information as well as money, to pursue non-fiscal purposes such as health checks on imported animals. Public agencies designed to monitor child malnutrition in a poor country can be reprogrammed to monitor child obesity and excessive calorie intake when affluence results in a child obesity problem rather than a child malnutrition one, as has happened in Singapore.

As with piecemeal adjustment, no completely new special machinery is introduced to vary behaviour. The dramatic effect is produced by a set of minor adjustments to each of a number of existing procedures, operations or control sites, perhaps originally established for quite different purposes to those now being served. Certainly, there is no theoretical necessity for the various operational units whose routines represent the parts of the overall reprogramming to be consciously aware of any change in purpose or overall product. 'They simply go on doing the job they are skilled and specialized in, emptying their in-trays as usual' (Dunsire, 1980, p. 33). Thus, like piecemeal adjustment, reprogramming requires no deep 'understanding' at operational level, though it may involve considerable design sophistication.

Recombination can operate in terms of implements as well as of routines more narrowly conceived. For instance, the control of business activities involves a number of familiar administrative implements – cash inducements, 'propaganda' (education, exhortation, information), authority (licences, certificates, quotas, prohibitions), direct action (storage, processing, transportation). The relative emphasis of those implements shifts over time, with different elements becoming dominant as circumstances change.

Similarly, the familiar set of implements can be continually adapted to new contexts. For instance, the basic tool-kit of business regulation can be applied in principle to any conceivable kind of enterprise. I have argued elsewhere (Hood, 1983, pp. 8, 119–20, 130–1) that administrative adaptation would be an infinitely more painful and intellectually demanding process than it actually is if completely new instruments had to be fashioned for each new problem as it comes along – be it technological innovations (such as cases (7) and (8)) or social fads and fashions (such as case (5), which is inspired by the movie-fuelled youth cults of the early 1980s). As it is, the mixture can be quite drastically altered without changing the basic ingredients.

Executed properly, recombination is an adaptive response which can combine economy in administrative materials, speed and an impression of effortlessness, in the sense that major overall changes result with hardly any noticeable change in operations. But compared to simple design variation, it taxes administrative 'system knowledge' and engineering skills to a much higher degree. Unless *all* of the minor adjustments involved in a reprogramming operation are specified and synchronised exactly, the result may be major disruption and chaos, as in the Pressman and Wildavsky implementation problem described in section V of the last chapter.

(3) Imitation

Imitation is the copying of a basic design which has shown itself to be workable elsewhere – another place, another operational context. For instance, in cases (1), (2) and (5), it may well be that T or C or D can simply adopt solutions devised elsewhere to the battery disposal problem or the traffic congestion problem or the stilt-wheeling problem. Why go to the effort of reinventing the wheel when there is a working model that can be copied?

Imitation is often thought of as intellectually inferior to solving a problem from scratch. But it can be a highly creative process. In engineering, for instance, it often takes real flair to see how a technique which has been designed for one context (such as epicyclic gears, originally devised for steering tanks in the early years of this century) can be put into another context (such as automobile automatic gearboxes or bicycle hub gears). Administrative 'engineering' abounds with similar examples – for instance, in using techniques originally devised for conciliating railway freight rate disputes to conciliating labour–management disputes (Hood, 1983, p. 130).

Like piecemeal adjustment, an imitative approach to adaptation may reduce risk by building on what is known. It may limit the administrative 'engineering' capacity needed, though few imitations are entirely straightforward. But, unlike piecemeal adjustment and recombination, copying another design wholesale (or with modifications) often means at some point that there will be a degree of disruption and 'down time' in the production process before the new system is switched on,

. if it is replacing some pre-existing way of doing things.

The importance of imitation is well established in writing about adaptation and indeed it is one of the commonest ways of changing administrative operations (I have discussed this elsewhere: see Hood, 1983, pp. 128–30). Much of the fascination of administrative history lies in tracing how the contacts and life experience of particular people cause design principles to be lifted from one context and put in another; and how design principles become diffused into new contexts. British public administration, for example, is full of borrowed designs. In the nineteenth century, the Scottish system of registering births, deaths and marriages was modelled on the French system, and land tenure administration modelled on the Irish system (Gibson, 1985, pp. 15–18, 26, 38). The old English system of land registration and measurement for property taxation was borrowed by the Normans from the Byzantine Empire. British stamp taxes were borrowed from the Netherlands in the seventeenth century, corporate and capital gains taxes from the USA in the 1960s, the 1973 sales tax from the 1920 French *paiement fractionnée* system, with a few indigenous modifications (Hood, 1985, pp. 22–3).

(4) Prototyping

Prototyping is the creation of an original design 'all at once' as a self-contained and purpose-built unit. Straight borrowing or slow cumulative variations in established designs do not count as prototyping in this sense. But certainly it is hard to draw a clear-cut boundary-line between prototyping and recombination – putting existing routines or implements together in a new way to achieve a different purpose.

Absolutely pure cases of administrative prototyping in these terms are rare, for reasons that are easy to understand. We might very well expect considerations of practicality and caution to lie *against* prototyping as the alternative to imitation in circumstances where a new design cannot be introduced by stages or by reprogramming existing sets of routines. Unavoidably, prototyping makes heavy demands on administrative engineering capacity. It often involves substantial 'down time' during trial and error or in the process of superseding the old design and putting the prototype into production. Prototyping in its nature tends to involve heavy start-up costs, high risk, likelihood of mistakes, delay and false starts (embarrassing initial failures which force designers back to the drawing-board).

Perhaps the classic argument on the advantages of imitation over prototyping was set out in 1915 by Thorstein Veblen, in the context of Imperial Germany's relatively late start in the Industrial Revolution; and the same general argument can be made in the narrower context of administrative development. Veblen pointed out that being second can have its advantages as well as its disadvantages. As he put it (Veblen, 1966, p. 24) 'as a matter of history, technological innovations and creations of an institutional nature have in many cases reached their fullest serviceability only at the hands of other communities and other peoples than those to whom these cultural elements owed their origin and initial success.'

Not only, he pointed out (ibid., 97), can imitators quickly and cheaply take over that which the prototyper has slowly and painfully developed over a long period. The imitator can also combine straight imitation with piecemeal adjustment, leaping straight to the most advanced form or logical extreme of the prototyper's art, unhampered by obsolescent equipment and skills and other encumbrances which may attach themselves to the prototypers' development in the original example. The prototyper is left with the development costs, and the imitator reaps the benefits.

As an example, Veblen (ibid., 130) gave the case of the small freight cars used in the British railway system (originally modelled on wagons used in coal mines before steam power was developed). In imitating the prototype British rail system, rail developers in other countries could dispense with what with hindsight could be seen to be the unduly narrow gauge of the British system. But it would have been extremely expensive and laborious for the British rail operators themselves to move from the original narrow gauge to a broader gauge, and impossible to make such a change in a piecemeal adjustment style.

Of course, prototyping can have its benefits, too, as Veblen did not deny. To the extent that there are enforceable intellectual property rights, the successful prototyper has a means of recovering his investment and appropriating the benefits to himself by charges on imitators or other means. The problem, of course, lies in the enforceability of such intellectual property rights. That is difficult enough even in ordinary business (given that the imitator can typically use rule category ambiguity to his advantage by minor modifications to the original design); and even more so in the field of public or government services. Tax designs, for instance, typically do not lend themselves to patent or intellectual property rights at all, and the same obviously applies all the more to military innovations, which can be quickly imitated by strategic opponents and used against the prototyper. It took the Germans three centuries of close contact with the Roman Empire to turn Roman infantry techniques to advantage against their colonial masters, but in the imitation of military radar in the 1940s they were only months behind the prototyping British (Steinbruner, 1974, p. 40). When the prototyper's lead is as foreshortened as in the latter case, a lot has to be at stake to make it worth while.

Moreover, prototyping might well be preferred to feasible alternative modes of innovation (imitation of an existing design, and the like) for reasons of prestige, empire-building or similar producer-group opportunism. Apart from being more interesting and challenging to the person on the job, a more prosaically self-regarding reason for preferring prototype work by employees or contractors is that the work of developing prototype designs tends to require more high-level personnel than does copying or elaboration of an existing design. In addition, yardsticks of the amount of funds and time needed to produce a new design from scratch will tend to be indeterminate, giving an opportunity for prototypers to escape from firm, experience-based oversight. For instance, the British Atomic Energy Authority for several decades strongly resisted pressure to imitate US-designed nuclear power plants rather than developing British-specific prototypes, since the producer-group interest of a scientific bureaucracy obviously favoured the second approach. The equivalent French bureaucracy switched to a strategy of imitation in 1969, but the British AEA was able to hold out for prototyping for another 10 years after that (the story is told in Williams, 1980).

Third, there may be circumstances in which there is really no alternative to prototyping. There may be no suitable prototype to copy, no scope for adjusting the existing system piecemeal, no possibility of achieving a desired result by recombining existing elements. In those 'rocket to the moon' circumstances, someone has to go first. In case (1), T might be the first town to run into serious mercury poisoning problems from disposal of batteries. In case (5), D might be the first or only country to be gripped by stilt-wheeling fever; and so on.

Naisbitt (1982, pp. 6–7) reports, for instance, that five states in the USA tend to be prototypers in matters of social invention, and that the other 45 are imitators. This applies to matters such as the initiation of local crime-watch groups or the development of hospices for the terminally ill. In Europe, prototype tax designs have tended to be developed by countries at the zenith of imperial vigour, when there was no suitable 'advanced country' model to copy (Roman/French sales taxes, Dutch stamp taxes, the British income tax). The same applies in extreme situations when imitation is ruled out by communications barriers. For instance, in case (3), there is not likely to be time to look into what has been done in other places in similar circumstances (unless it so happens that there is someone on the spot with experience of a comparable case). Action has to be taken immediately. It is no accident that the only two 'pure' (or nearly pure) British tax prototype designs of the last 50 years – namely, Purchase Tax in 1940 and the 1944 Pay As You Earn scheme for withholding income tax from employees' wages on a cumulative basis over the tax year

Table 5.1: Responses to change: Four modes

| | | 'Down time' (or potential disruption to existing operations) | |
		Low	High
administrative engineering capacity	Low	Cell-splitting ('Start from where you are')	Imitation ('Borrow a working model')
	High	Recombination ('Vary the mix')	Prototyping ('Start from scratch')

(Cmnd. 6734, 1976, pp. 21–9; Kay and King, 1980, p. 20) – were both developed within the highly insular confines of a beleaguered war economy, when international communications on tax matters were necessarily limited.

Table 5.1 summarizes the four methods that have been discussed in this section as ways of changing public service provision. It also indicates the extent to which the four approaches to innovation can in general be expected to test administrative engineering capacity or system knowledge, and to introduce disruption in existing operations. If we want to limit the cost of adaptation in terms of the engineering knowledge and skill required to bring it about, we should normally prefer piecemeal adjustment and imitation to recombination and prototyping. If we want to limit the cost of adaptation in terms of disruption to existing operations in replacing some current system by an alternative one, we should normally prefer piecemeal adjustment and recombination to imitation and prototyping. Prototyping tends to be in the 'high cost' box in both dimensions. In practice, of course, most administrative adaptation involves some hybrid of the four 'pure' approaches discussed here.

IV. DISPOSITION TO RESPOND

Failure to adapt may spring from not registering or wrongly diagnosing change in demand or production possibilities for public services. It may spring from inability to vary behaviour, either because of a real lack of options or because of a failure to think in new terms. But what if failure to respond appropriately to change stems not from genuine blindness or intellectual puzzlement, but rather from emotional conservatism, vanity, groupthink, lassitude or vested interest?

That, of course, brings in the third element of adaptation which was outlined in section I. That is some motivation to adapt, or some selection process which punishes inappropriate responses and rewards appropriate ones. To many, this is the real issue in making public services adaptive. For instance, it is sometimes said that many public services are like an Ibsen play or a Schubert trio in that the 'product' stays the same as it was when first designed, and so do the methods used to make it (Heald, 1983, pp. 114–15). Peacock (1979) claims that this is not due to unchanging demand or a real absence of different ways of providing such services (factors which are sometimes invoked to explain the 'Ibsen play effect'). It springs mainly, Peacock argues, from rule structures which do not provide effective *incentives* for changing methods of service provision.

To this way of thinking, the important thing is to get the incentive structure right and then the other problems will look after themselves. The rule factors instanced by economic analysts like Peacock as creating incentives to adapt include the degree to which competition sets up pressures to keep up to date, the extent to which tax-based provision blanks out signals about changing demand and supply conditions, the extent to which transferability of ownership punishes failure to adapt, the extent to which individual employees stand to gain from adaptation in services or to lose from failure to adapt.

Now this, of course, takes us back to the six design issues in organizing public services which were discussed in the last chapter. Space does not permit us to go over that ground again, to look at the way that design of organization might affect incentives to adapt. The reader must be left to do that for him- or herself. Table 5.2 summarizes some arguments in common currency on the matter (especially those emanating from the 'public choice' stable), to set the reader thinking about this. As Table 5.2 indicates, arguments in common currency suggest that most forms of organization have some possible advantages in adaptation; and that in deciding among them, much depends on what dimension of adaptation is held to be most important; which in turn depends on the specific problem at issue. It suggests that we should be wary of all-purpose formulae for adaptive organization.

Of course, concentrating on the way that rules shape incentives to adapt in this way is to ignore all the imponderables of personality, morale, social psychology. This is a conventional neglective fiction. But obviously, such factors may cut across the expected effects of a rule structure in individual cases.

Moreover – to repeat a point made in the last chapter – once we move from the extremes (all the right-hand features or all the left-hand features of Table 5.2) to the 4093 intermediate possible compounds, prediction becomes harder and arguments less clear-cut. For instance, the argument that the 'monopoly tax-financed public bureau' is peculiarly resistant to adaptation is so familiar as to be a cliché (see, for instance, Crozier, 1964, p. 196; Beer, 1975, p. 105). But in practice, as was argued in the last chapter, we do not choose only between 'monopoly tax-financed public bureau' versus 'rival user charge-financed private enterprise' for the provision of public services. Once we come to the many hybrids which don't fit that simple dichotomy, the standard argument doesn't tell us what to expect.

For instance, what happens when user-charge finance is combined with monopoly, as commonly applies to power utilities? Here, there are quite strong incentives to respond to change, if failure to do so will reduce revenue from users, but the incentives are skewed towards making changes which transfer costs from producer to consumer. Alternatively, what happens when general tax funding is combined with competition, as sometimes occurs when rival military units (army, navy, air force) compete as alternative possible suppliers of particular defence facilities? Here again, there are real incentives to adapt to keep up with the competition, especially in ways which swell rather than cut budgetary resources – by inventing new tasks, more sophisticated or higher quality methods or equipment for performing existing tasks. Once we move to hybridization of the six dimensions of organization considered earlier, effects on adaptiveness quickly become indeterminate.

V. SUMMARY AND CONCLUSION

This chapter has distinguished capacity to detect change, capacity to respond to change, and the incentive to respond to change. These are not necessarily the same thing, as is suggested on Table 5.2.

For instance, general tax finance coupled with monopoly and large scale may mean weak incentives to adapt quickly to environmental change, as orthodox argument stresses. But it

Table 5.2: Adaptation and organizational choice: Some arguments in common currency

Dimension 1	*Do-it-yourself*	*Specialized provision*
Detection capacity	Wearer knows where shoe pinches?	Specialists know best about changing production functions?
Response capacity	Slack resources available to handle crises?	Specialist community fosters imitation?
Motivation to change	Self-help motivation to adapt services?	Vested interests in existing supply patterns?
Dimension 2	*Small scale*	*Large scale*
Detection capacity	Short lines from producers to consumers?	More resources for forecasting and analysis?
Response capacity	Little spare capacity in crisis?	Able to concentrate resources on a single point in crises?
Motivation to change		Experiment difficult, change implementation traumatic?
Dimension 3	*Performance contract*	*Direct employment*
Detection capacity		
Response capacity	Inflexible unless all contingencies foreseen?	'Order of the day' can change direction at any time?
Motivation to change	Depends on contract terms?	Employees on fixed salaries cannot recoup individual financial gains from adaptation, nor suffer losses from failure to adapt unless enterprise closes down?

	Multiple provider	*Single provider*
Dimension 4		
Detection capacity	Risk that no one sees 'the whole picture', but assumptions, etc. rigorously tested?	Risk of distortion?
Response capacity	Larger pool of available routines for imitation?	Easier to recoup costs of prototyping?
Motivation to change	Competitive pressure may spur change, 'holdout' possibilities in non-rival structures hold it back?	
Dimension 5	*User-charge finance*	*General tax finance*
Detection capacity	Price mechanism signals change in demand and cost?	
Response capacity	Financial incentives to cut costs and fill new niches?	Ability to pump in resources in crises?
Motivation to change		
Dimension 6	*Private/independent enterprise*	*Public bureaucracy*
Detection capacity		
Response capacity		
Motivation to change	Transferability of ownership rights penalizes lack of response?	Permanence aids piecemeal adjustment?

may also mean strong capacity to respond, especially to a crisis or lethal discontinuity, which can only be coped with by drawing on slack – resources which are ordinarily redundant or surplus to essential requirements (Beer, 1966, pp. 197–8). Access to general tax funds may avoid revenue constraints that could otherwise cripple adaptation, for instance in conditions of falling demand (see Hirschman, 1970). A monopoly's 'fat' or spare capacity can be drawn upon to cope with lethal discontinuities (such as the telephone cable failure case, mentioned in section III, where surplus staff could be used as (say) fire-watchers on top of tall buildings to replace the lost telephone-based system of summoning emergency services). Large scale may enable a heavy concentration of resources to be brought to a single point in an emergency. Large scale coupled with monopoly may make it possible to insure or carry back-up capacity for major risks with a low probability of occurring (the essence of many lethal discontinuities), in a way that cost pressures might well prevent in competitive or small-scale organization.

In fact, likening public service provision to an Ibsen play or Schubert trio is an analogy which conceals as much as it reveals. As we saw in section I, pressures to change the script or the performance are rarely absent (perhaps because many public services, like the law, have to be ready to deal with every case). And as we saw in section III, there are a number of quite well-understood ways of altering the performance, some at least of which are usually available.

When it comes to motivation to adapt – the central question in the eyes of the 'public choice' school – the issues discussed in the last chapter over choice of organization come back into the picture. The next chapter in part continues that theme, by reviewing the prospects for designing 'consumer-driven' (rather than producer-driven) public services.

QUESTIONS FOR REVIEW

1. The Magnifico Dam is a new prestige project. It is paid for from taxes and operated by the Magnifico Dam Administration, a large public bureaucracy with some

20,000 employees. MDA spends a lot on PR to present an image of a model enterprise and counter criticism of its operations. At present, MDA is in the middle of a set of delicate negotiations, because:

(a) a request for money to build the Magnifico Phase II project is being considered by funding authorities;

(b) MDA's operating budget is under scrutiny after an employee dismissed by MDA publicly criticized the enterprise as employing too many management staff and spending too much on entertainment, conferences abroad and executive suites; and

(c) MDA's manual workers have threatened to strike unless a large pay claim is met in full.

One day, a junior manual worker on a routine maintenance inspection sees large cracks appearing in part of the wall of the main dam. In the light of the discussion of organizational choices in the last chapter, consider the obstacles that might lie in the way of top-level recognition of this change and of swift action to deal with it.

2. Suppose that a breakthrough in pig-breeding research has produced *porcus volaticus*. *Porcus volaticus* can fly quite long distances at heights of up to 800 feet (244 m). Suggest,

(a) how to control movement of *porcus volaticus* in order to contain disease within a small area in the event of an outbreak of foot and mouth or swine vesicular disease;

(b) how to apply international animal movement controls and quarantine arrangements to these animals;

(c) how to prevent damage and navigational hazards to aircraft from being caused by these animals.

3. Suppose it has been decided to limit the ability of sportsmen, dancers, film stars and other celebrities to promote fitness courses and aerobic dance or exercise programmes (on the grounds that lack of attention paid to the health risks for unfit middle-aged people may cause

avoidable deaths through heart attacks, etc.). What kind of administrative innovation would this require?

4. Do you think that competition in public service provision will lead services to be adapted more quickly to changes in demand than would apply in a single-provider structure? How do you think a system of multiple but non-rival producers would compare with a monopoly provider in this respect?

GUIDE TO FURTHER READING

Beer (1966) and Deutsch (1963) discuss administrative adaptation from a cybernetic viewpoint. Nelson and Winter (1982) discuss adaptation in the context of economic theory. From a quite different intellectual tradition and set of starting assumptions, empirical organizational–sociology studies of enterprises have tended to highlight the special difficulties that tax-financed public bureaucracies encounter in responding to change. Useful sources include Crozier (1964) and Perrow (1979).

The theory of administrative 'reprogramming', as discussed in section III, was originally expounded by Dunsire 1978a, Chapter 7, but is more clearly explained in Dunsire 1980, pp. 9–54. A discussion of administrative 'learning' and 'counter-learning' is contained in Hood (1976, pp. 74–93).

6 Consumer Sovereignty and Convenience Administration

'You can have any colour you like as long as it's black.' (Henry Ford)

For a century or so, most theory about public service provision took public bureaucracy as its point of departure and was about how to perfect such bureaucracies. (The modern classics in this vein are the works of Wilson (1887) and Weber, in Gerth and Mills, 1948, p. 214.) Such theory tended to assume that public services were (or should be) normally provided by politically-directed hierarchies of permanent, full-time, functionally specialized government officials, wielding the public power as fiduciary trustees for some wider group of beneficiaries. The problem was how to shape the structure, staffing and operating rules of the full-time government employment apparatus so as to ensure that public bureaucracy worked smoothly and effectively.

The answer, in much writing in this vein, was to set sensible working boundaries within and between bureaucracies ('sensible' usually meant cutting out rivalry and overlap) and to build up the expertise, specialization and dedication of public bureaucrats. The recipe usually included better (or at least more) training and professionalism – meaning specialized technical expertise and skills in general decision-making and planning. Heavy emphasis was laid on what Martin (1983, p. 18) calls 'the aggrandizement of management', within a framework of public bureaucracy service provision. Such an approach is 'producerist', in that it starts with those who are taken to be the producers of public services, rather than with consumers. The assumption is that the standard recipes for making public bureaucracies better will ultimately result in better services for consumers.

169

That 'paradigm' of what administrative analysis ought to be about has by no means disappeared. It is strongly entrenched in institutes of public service development and training all round the world. But there are other possible starting-points for analysing public service provision, which are just as 'classical' in their standing as the Wilson/Weber approach.

That is, we might start by putting the spotlight on the public service user or consumer rather than on the producing 'practitioner'. We might start by looking at public services from the ground up, not from the nature of rulership, bureaucracy or management in general. We might take public bureaucracy in its classical form as one – but only one – possible form of provision among others, not the starting-point and defining field of analysis. Instead of aiming for public officials with the integrity and wisdom of Plato's philosopher king, we might aim for a system in which quality of service does not depend very much on managers of exceptional talent or on man's more heroic qualities (Niskanen, 1971, p. 184). In general, we might try to design a framework of rules that reward public service producers for meeting the preferences of consumers and punish them for not doing so, rather than giving the producers the job of deciding as trustees what beneficiaries ought to want in the way of quality, quantity and cost of services provided. Looked at from this point of view, providing public services is not necessarily to be equated with polishing up public bureaucracies.

Indeed, if there is a 'theory' of public administration embedded in Anglo-Saxon economics and common law – which are in general anti-*étatist*, cool on bureaucracy, and individualist in orientation (even when it comes to the 'public power') – these would seem to be the basic assumptions from which it starts. Two classical authors who looked at the 'public service problem' from these backgrounds (Adam Smith and Jeremy Bentham) certainly worked on those assumptions. That tradition has enjoyed a notable revival in theorizing about public service provision over the past 20 years or so. No student of public administration today can ignore it, even though the producer-orientated, bureaucracy-centred, fiduciary-trustee tradition remains strong.

Of course, both approaches have their limits. The second in

particular raises interesting questions about how far a principle of 'consumer sovereignty' might feasibly be taken in public service provision. This is the subject of this final chapter. It goes back over ground which has been traversed since the start of the book, and the treatment is necessarily speculative and brief. The chapter is in three parts. First, we explore how far a principle of 'consumer sovereignty' could be taken in public service provision. The second part looks at the case against maximum feasible consumer sovereignty. The third part briefly considers 'convenience administration' or a 'user-friendly' style of service provision, as an alternative to pure consumer sovereignty.

I. CONSUMER SOVEREIGNTY IN PUBLIC SERVICE PROVISION: POSSIBILITIES AND LIMITS

How far is it feasible to apply consumer sovereignty to public services? Can those services be made to respond to the demands and convenience of consumers, as *seen* by those consumers, rather than to the judgements and preferences of producers? 'Consumer sovereignty' may be an attractive-seeming slogan. But earlier chapters should have made the reader aware of the limits to which it could be taken, even in theory, in providing public service. This section briefly goes over those limits.

Before you can be 'sovereign consumer' in the fullest sense, at least four conditions must be met:

(a) You can choose among a number of suppliers concentrated into a conveniently small area and competing for your custom.
(b) You can choose among a number of goods or services of varying quality, design and cost.
(c) While attempts may well be made to influence your choice, and some limits may be placed on what may be legally bought and sold, you are generally taken to be the best judge of your own interests. You must decide what items will best serve your needs and what is a reasonable price to pay for them. If you are foolish or gullible, you have to take the consequences.

(d)   You may choose not to buy at all. You are not literally coerced into making a purchase.

As everyone knows, it is rare for all of these conditions to be met in full in any transaction. Sometimes we may come fairly close to them, for instance, when we shop in a fresh-food market which contains many rival stalls, each selling the same general class of goods. But it is also fairly rare to find ourselves at the opposite extreme, where *none* of those conditions is met. Of course, it does happen sometimes. Suppose that you are lying in the street, injured, unconscious and in urgent need of medical help, in a town which has only one doctor. In this case:

(a)   Only one supplier for the service you need is available to you.

(b)   The quality of service has to be taken as given and uniform.

(c)   The service provider decides what kind of service you need, and at what price to sell it to you. (In fact, in such a case, a law court would probably write a retrospective contract for the service if the doctor demanded too extortionate a price for his services. But let us ignore that complication here.)

(d)   You are forced to buy. You literally cannot walk away from the supplier.

As a matter of fact, public services vary a good deal in where they come in the range between total consumer sovereignty and complete producer sovereignty. They also vary in the amount of consumer sovereignty that is *in principle* possible. Those two things, of course, are not the same. Consumer sovereignty may be – and frequently is – denied where competition to supply is feasible, but monopoly is chosen; where variation in quality of service is possible but uniformity is imposed; where it might be possible for the individual consumer to choose what he wants, but the choice is made for him; where a consumer could decline to buy, but is coerced into 'buying' a service, whether he wants it or not. Let us briefly review the scope for 'consumer sovereignty' in public services.

(1) Choice of Suppliers

For many public services, it is in principle quite feasible to let the consumer choose among a number of suppliers. The argument is only about whether such an arrangement is desirable, as in the case of radio-stations. Much of the work of the 'public choice' school, referred to in Chapter 4, is about how competition for supply and consumer choice can be designed into public service provision. A favourite device of such work is voucher schemes which give transferable entitlements to consume particular services, such as college education, garbage collection, medical care.

But for some public services, monopoly is unavoidable. We encountered one standard example – piped water-supply – in Chapter 1. Local telephone service is another. Of course, the other three conditions of consumer sovereignty may still apply even when there is only one supplier. The consumer may still be able to decide what quantity or quality of service to buy – the amount of time he spends on the telephone, the type of telephone apparatus he rents. His tastes may be broadly accepted as given. He may even be able to elect not to buy, for instance if he decides to do without telephones or electricity or piped water. Even a monopoly supplier can be put under some pressure from its customers under a user-charge and varied menu of service regime, but of course these pressures in practice get weaker the more practically indispensable the service is to the ordinary consumer. Where user-charge customers cannot feasibly opt out from using a monopoly service even temporarily, they have to rely on using what Hirschman (1970) calls 'voice' – i.e. complain, campaign, ask for the manager, demonstrate, browbeat. As everyone knows, such tactics are highly uncertain in their effects.

For genuine natural monopolies, the maximum feasible consumer sovereignty is for consumers as a group from time to time to choose the single supplier from rival candidates for the job. That is, the operation of such services can be based on limited-term franchises or contracts, as with (say) local cable TV provision. This follows the Chadwickian principle of 'competition for the field' rather than simultaneous rival supply *in* the field (see Chapter 4, section V). This principle has been resuscitated by modern public choice theorists such as

Demsetz (1968). Demsetz proposed limited-term franchises for all monopoly public utilities, with allocation on the basis of sealed bids on price and quality invited from potential suppliers.

Theoretically, of course, this principle need not be confined to user-charge utilities, though Demsetz stopped there. It could be applied to non-user charge natural monopoly services as well, and sometimes is. But choosing public service suppliers by periodic contracts is attended by well-known difficulties. First, what competition to supply there is will inevitably consist of rival estimates and promises rather than of finished goods or services actually on offer for inspection. It is then a fine exercise in judgement as to how to weigh the credibility of proposals that look very attractive on paper but may very well not be matched by sufficient financial reserves or experience in the field. Second, an incumbent contractor or franchise often has a powerful advantage in practice over rivals in such allocative exercises (see Hood, 1976, pp. 31–50; Breyer, 1982, pp. 92–3). Third, a franchisee who reneges on his obligations at a strategic moment is often in a powerful position to force retrospective renegotiation of the terms of the contract, especially if he is insolvent and court actions for damages would be fruitless. Fourth, genuine rivalry among potential suppliers is notoriously difficult to engineer; a point noted by Adam Smith, as we saw in Chapter 4.

Of course, even natural monopoly has its limits. There are not many world-wide natural monopolies. Often, the dissatisfied customer could in theory take his custom to another monopolist's territory. In principle, consumer sovereignty can be reconciled to some extent with natural monopoly provision by engineering the maximum possible decentralization and diversity of public service 'packages' in neighbouring districts.

This is, indeed, a principle commonly advocated by economics-based writers on public choice. Niskanen, one of the best-known contributors to that approach, claims that the monopoly problem in public service provision is not very serious when providers operate within relatively small territories, because dissatisfied customers can easily vote with their feet. He argues that 'the automobile and an efficient housing market are probably the strongest contributors to the responsiveness and efficiency of [US] local government' (Niskanen, 1971, p. 130). In the same vein, Macrae (1984, p. 103) forecasts a demand for increased choice in public services by local-level polls at which voters decide between varying packages of service quality and tax cost, preferably on a performance contract basis which obliges service providers to cut taxes if services do not reach a certain standard of performance on 'objective' tests (What would be the problem about writing such contracts?)

(2) Choice of Quality and Quantity of Services Consumed

To be fully 'sovereign', the consumer must be able to choose from a range of items of varying quality or quantity. For instance, different people have different tastes in telephone handsets. Some like the strictly functional, no-nonsense variety. Some like them modelled in the shape of Snoopy or Mickey Mouse. Others prefer reproduction antiques, in the style of the telephones their great-grandparents used, and so on. For years, the British telephone monopoly responded to consumer demand for variety in handsets by simply forbidding subscribers to use anything other than a standard utilitarian handset. Only in 1981 after considerable evasion of this rule by subscribers defiantly using non-standard handsets from private suppliers, was the law changed to reflect the existence of diverse tastes, and to accept the principle of customer choice of handset, so long as basic technical standards were met (cf. Cmnd. 8610, 1982).

Many might see this as a tale of the times. Naisbitt (1982, p. 232) says, 'In today's Baskins – Robbins society, everything comes in at least 31 flavors.' *Everything*? Can we have '31 flavors' in public services?

Choice of quality and quantity is indeed quite feasible for some public services. For instance, where there are user-charges, consumers can be given the option of more expensive de luxe service or cheaper utilitarian service – express versus regular mail delivery service, first class or economy class transport. Often, too, a range of alternative services may be offered, for instance in educational programmes in schools.

But some public services are consumed collectively not individually and cannot be otherwise. The flood-control case with which we started is one. That means that consumers cannot individually decide the type and quality of service that they want (as they can with mail services), but only as part of a collectivity. At best, we can only have 'collective consumer sovereignty' in such cases. And even putting that into effect raises very well-known collective-choice difficulties, as we saw right at the outset. What if some consumers in V want lower-quality flood control and water supply at correspondingly low cost (that is, they prefer lower taxes and charges, coupled with higher flood risks, higher risks of water-supply breakdowns, lower water pressure, lower water purity, lower and more depersonalized service quality) and others have the opposite preferences, wanting high quality and individualized service at high cost? '31 flavors' simply can't be offered here. Whatever is decided, some consumers will complain about it.

Indeed, part of the problem posed by pure public goods is the built-in conflict between general interest in keeping total tax costs down and the interest of each individual user in getting the highest possible quality of service. Whoever produces such services will inevitably find themselves justifying poor service quality to dissatisfied customers in terms of the need to keep overall tax costs down, and at the same time justifying high demands for tax funds to budget allocators in terms of the need to provide service of acceptable quality. For the opportunist, of course, such a situation is ripe for exploitation. To some extent, the same goes for joint-consumption services (such as water supply, telephone lines) in which service quality, in some aspects at least, must be uniform. High producer/consumer conflict can be endemic in such services, given that production costs can usually be cut by raising compliance costs or user costs, or by producing completely standard rather than individualized service.

As in the telephone handsets case, private supplementation may be one way of rescuing consumer sovereignty for a joint-consumption service. For instance, some aspects of water supply are subject to inescapable joint consumption by all users, but other aspects may lend themselves to private supplementation. Suppose that some people in V intensely want fluoridized water, but others are implacably opposed to fluoridization; or that some only want water that is safe to drink from the tap but others want water that is pleasant-tasting (involving extra costs in water softening, etc.). If minimum quality non-fluoridized water is supplied to everyone, individual consumers can put fluoride tablets in their water tanks if they want to, or install water softeners to bring up the quality of the water to the standard which they prefer. Private supplementation is quite often possible for services which in some respects involve joint consumption, even for law enforcement, as we saw in Chapter 3. (For a discussion of private supplementation, see Brennan and Pincus, in Taylor, 1983, pp. 33–49).

Of course, private supplementation is not always feasible for joint-consumption services. In that case (as for natural monopolies), the only other way to bring in some degree of consumer sovereignty is through variety in quality and cost of provision in different geographical areas, so that users can take such factors into account in deciding where to live. But there are several practical difficulties with that approach to consumer choice. One of them is a problem of enforcement and opportunism, of a kind that should now be familiar. That is, what if opportunists in large numbers choose to live in a low-cost/low-service tax district just next door to a high-cost/high-service tax district, such that they are able to benefit from the services provided in the latter area (e.g. lavish public parks, reference libraries, and the like) in respect of services in which exclusion is infeasible or expensive?

Making public services respond to consumer preferences thus becomes problematic:

(a) Where the service unavoidably involves joint consumption.
(b) Where consumers have conflicting preferences about content or quality of provision or when there is some genuine ambiguity about exactly who is to be defined as a user or consumer, (e.g. are school users to be defined as schoolchildren or parents or employers or the community at large? And what about prisons?)
(c) Where private supplementation of service cannot be used

to reconcile varying or conflicting tastes about price or quality.

(d)   Where dissatisfied customers cannot easily exit to another joint-supply unit.

(3) Consumer or User as Best Judge of his Own Interests

The 'sovereign' consumer is taken to be the best judge of his own interests. This is closely related to the last principle. Again, in many public services it is quite possible to accept consumers' tastes as given. For instance, instead of rigidly prescribing course combinations according to what educators in their wisdom think to be a balanced study programme, colleges can operate like self-service stores, with their customers free to pick course units in any quantity, combination or sequence whatever. Instead of providing a diet of high-minded programmes deemed to be suitable for viewers and listeners, broadcasters can provide material which simply responds to mass preference. Both colleges and broadcasting institutions in western countries have in fact tended to move in the direction of 'consumer sovereignty' in matters of taste in the recent past.

But the dictum that 'the customer is always right' cannot be applied to many public services. Wildavsky (1979, pp. 155–83) describes how ideas of 'merit wants' – taking some wants as more deserving than others – have crept in to economic discussion of one field of public policy after another, supplanting the 'consumer sovereignty' idea that all tastes are equally meritorious. As we shall see in the next section, one of the arguments for fiduciary trusteeship rather than consumer sovereignty in public service provision is that the general run-of-the-mill consumers of many services simply do not have the knowledge necessary for evaluating the options, for instance in the selection of safe aircraft to travel in.

Where intelligent consumer choice is hampered by lack of knowledge, must the consumer's choice be made for him on some fiduciary principle? Not necessarily. In such cases it may be possible partly to rescue consumer sovereignty by compulsory disclosure rules. Such rules compel producers to give information to consumers which will enable the latter to make more informed choices. An example is the old Chinese rule that physicians must display the number of patients who have died in their care, so that prospective patients have something to go on in choosing a physician. Instead of deciding whether or not to allow the public sale of items which might be dangerous in some circumstances (with all the intractable difficulties that such a choice usually involves), we might simply require that prospective buyers are made aware (say) that the product contains a food additive which produced a 0.1 per cent rise in the rate of spontaneous mutation when fed in concentrated amounts to laboratory mice over three months. Let the customer agonize over what to do in the light of such information, rather than foreclosing his choice (see Breyer, 1982, pp. 161–4).

But obviously, there are sharp practical limits to the extent to which customers' deficiencies in relevant knowledge can be remedied by mandatory disclosure, for instance in evaluating reactor safety in different types of nuclear power plants. Economists have always seen this as a way in which free markets can break down. In those circumstances, one is inevitably thrown back either onto some fiduciary principle, or to an attempt to construct procedural rules to shape the way that 'expert' knowledge is brought to bear on the relevant decision (see Stone, 1975; Majone, in Weiss and Barton, 1980, pp. 235–58).

Moreover, even apart from that familiar problem, the principle of allowing the consumer to choose the kind of service he wants may have potentially difficult equity implications – a problem discussed further in section II. For instance, should people be able to design their own individual rules of procedure for the conduct of a decision, hearing or even court case affecting them? Mashaw (1983, p. 97) discusses this in the context of the way that claims for disability benefits are handled in the US Disability Programme. Some claimants might prefer their case to be handled in strict confidence, for instance, if embarrassing bowel disorders or the like are in question. But others might believe that they will be denied justice unless their hearing takes place in open court. Some might want an inquisitorial hearing, others an adversarial one, and so on. How far can procedures in such cases be customized to fit consumers' preferences without undermining the principle of equal treatment of similar cases?

(4) Ability to Opt Out

The 'sovereign' consumer is free not to buy at all, unlike the unconscious person lying in the street in need of medical care. For services which are not pure public goods, it is possible to fund the service by user-charges which give an 'opt-out' facility. In practice, of course, many such services (like schools) are paid for out of taxes rather than user-charges, so that non-users or those dissatisfied with the service cannot opt out of paying for it, even if they can opt out of using it. Often, the denial of 'opt out' possibilities in such cases rests on equity grounds, to be discussed in section II.

When it comes to pure public goods, of course, we saw at the outset that if such services are to be provided at all, the right not to buy must be denied (except where voluntary provision will suffice or where it is in the interest of a single individual or a few people to provide the service for everybody). The problem, of course, arises when we pass from services which are quite clearly needed to save life (as with flood control, even though there may be differences of opinion over the quality of service required, as we have seen) to the more 'luxurious' kinds of public goods – decorative street lighting, monuments, weather control. As we saw in Chapter 1, the latter type of service has very high potential for generating conflict when a group of people with differing tastes is forced to consume as a collectivity.

II. THE CASE AGAINST CONSUMER SOVEREIGNTY

For some public services, as we have seen, full-blooded consumer sovereignty is impossible. But it is also clear that actual provision often stops well short even of such consumer sovereignty as is in principle possible. Can this ever be justified? What might be the case against maximum feasible consumer sovereignty as a design principle for public services?

There are five familiar lines of argument on which such a case might be based. They are:

(1)   The paternalistic case: reflecting, for instance, the distaste for 'philistine' popular prejudices (e.g. in art) or the belief

that the 'average' consumer is ill-equipped to make intelligent decisions, for instance in choosing among types of medical treatment.

(2) The belief that competition for supply will drive down standards – for instance, that standards of safety or quality will be driven down to the level of the least scrupulous supplier (the 'Gresham's Law' problem: see Chapter 4, section V).

(3) The belief that life must be made tolerable for those who provide the service – for instance, if too many optional classes in schools would mean more work, stress and exposure than teachers can reasonably be expected to cope with.

(4) The belief that the average cost of production will be lowered if the service 'product' is made uniform.

(5) The egalitarian belief that everyone ought to receive exactly the same quality or quantity of service, irrespective of what they are able or prepared to pay.

The Fiduciary Trustee Approach

No one would assert it as a principle that public service provision *ought* to be solely geared to serving the interests of the service producer, except when services are supplied by 'co-production'. (Of course, many assert that producer interests often come first in practice.) At most, it might be argued that keeping producers happy should be a subsidiary aim, or a necessary precondition for providing good service. This is argument (3) above.

Consumer sovereignty might also be rejected by the use of arguments (1) and (2). Public services, it may be held, are best provided by producers acting as fiduciary trustees, not as market traders dealing with sovereign consumers. Such producers must have a wide discretion to judge the best interests of their clients. Clients may not be able to judge their interests for themselves because they are hopelessly divided, lack the relevant expertise, or cannot be trusted to take a long view or to weigh risks properly. We have already looked briefly at the fiduciary principle in Chapter 4. It is in the nature of fiduciary trusteeship to act paternalistically, but the paternalism should properly be altruistic, not self-regarding.

Such a style of provision therefore relies heavily on the integrity and good judgement of 'high-minded and highly educated civil servants' (von Mises, 1944, p. v).

Strong claims have traditionally been made for the fiduciary trustee principle in fields such as education, technical services, town planning, public health. In the 1920s and 1930s, the idea of public service 'trusts' of this kind perhaps enjoyed its greatest acceptance. Even in the USA, with its individualist and anti-bureaucratic ethos, the philosophy of trusting the exercise of the public power to the discretion of (assumedly other-regarding) professionals or experts became well established in public administration and public law during the New Deal era, and remained so for several decades, especially in business regulation. In Europe it went even further. For instance, when radio broadcasting began in the 1920s, several European countries (notably the UK) entrusted the service to a monopoly public bureaucracy on the grounds that 'high-minded and highly educated' producers would provide programmes that they judged to be edifying and wholesome for the public at large, rather than simply responding to 'market demand'. That system survived in Britain for nearly 30 years and the ruins of it are still quite visible even now.

Now it is impossible even in theory to avoid such 'producer sovereignty' for services such as the custody of minor children, the confused elderly, the mentally ill, the dangerous criminal. This applies to much regulatory activity to deal with 'tragedy of the commons' cases, and the like. But in general, argument (1), as a case for fiduciary trusteeship rather than consumer choice public services is more often challenged today than it used to be, both in theory and practice.

It is impossible here to chart fully the way in which the stock of the fiduciary trustee approach has fallen. Perhaps it is only part of a more general waning of the mystiques of expertise once possessed by the professional classes, and of growing scepticism about the disinterestedness and altruism of such groups (see Rourke, in Weiss and Barton, 1980, p. 110; Pollitt, 1984). Even elected public officials are less trusted as fiduciary actors than they used to be (see Marshall, 1984, pp. 143–4). Today, the assertion of 'educational values' by educators may well be equated with the views of the Campbell Soup Company about the value of having soup for lunch (see Sowell, in Gatti, 1981, p. 48). But it was not always so. The declining force of argument (3), too, may reflect a wider decline in the status of producer groups, with a weakening in corporatist and labour union claims to special privileges, and the waxing of 'consumerism' as a political force in the USA and Europe in the 1970s.

The case for 'fiduciary trusteeship' in public services has weakened in intellectual terms as well as in practice. Much of that derives from the rediscovery of institutional analysis in economics, from roughly the mid-twentieth century onwards, and the recreation of theories of administration built on assumptions of public officials as self-regarding utilitarians, rather than altruistic fiduciaries. In the process, a new style of administrative analysis grew up outside the traditional disciplinary boundaries of 'public administration'. That subject is no longer the near-exclusive intellectual property of public lawyers and political scientists that it was 50 years ago. The development of ideas such as Leibenstein's (1976) theory of X-inefficiency in producer organization and Williamson's (1975) analysis of information-impactedness in hierarchies, sharply exposed some of the efficiency problems glossed over by comfortable assumptions about fiduciary behaviour in bureaucratic provision. Of course, the received public administration theory was developed in the late nineteenth and early twentieth centuries by people from a legal and political science background who had no real conception of allocative or X-efficiency (Albrow, 1970, p. 64). So it is not surprising that assumptions about efficiency should turn out to be the intellectual Achilles' heel of that approach.

For over 20 years, the traditional fiduciary trustee idea of public service provision has been exposed to a competing paradigm from economics-based 'public choice' writers, as described in Chapter 4. Such writers have concentrated on arguments about efficiency, contrasting the incentives set up for opportunistic producers and consumers under monopolized bureaucratic service provision with those set up by other modes of provision. At the same time, in administrative law, the deference shown to the discretionary exercise of the public power by 'experts', has been on the wane for a long time, particularly in the sphere of regulating business standards (see Freedman, 1978, p. 59; Hawkins, in Hawkins and Thomas, 1984, p. 4).

The Redistributive Case against Consumer Choice

The revolt against the 'fiduciary trustee' style of service provision has consisted mainly of declining acceptance of argument (1) as an all-purpose case against consumer sovereignty, and to some degree arguments (2) and (3) too. But the last argument (5), is perhaps the most commonly cited reason for restricting consumer sovereignty in public services (not that the others are especially uncommon). For consumer sovereignty to operate, income and wealth distribution, like tastes and preferences, are taken as given. The wealthy consumer is free to choose utilitarian or de luxe service, while the poorer consumer inevitably has to select the former – which may mean very little choice at all. If unequal distribution of income among consumers prevents real choice, does that not undermine the case for maximum feasible consumer sovereignty in public service provision?

Certainly, in circumstances where the vast mass of public service consumers live in grinding poverty and ignorance, at or near subsistence level, with perhaps a handful of wealthy people at the other end of the social scale, the equity case against consumer sovereignty has considerable force. The same will probably go for arguments (1), (2) and (3), in such conditions. But that decreasingly describes the social context in which public services are provided in economically developed countries, with an increasingly educated population, an income distribution pattern that increasingly bulges in the middle rather than at the bottom, and the vast majority of citizens living well above the subsistence level. This development may well be part of the reason for the waning of the 'fiduciary trustee' approach in such countries. Perhaps argument (5) becomes less convincing as an all-purpose case against consumer sovereignty in conditions of majority affluence.

Of course, even in the rich countries, large numbers of people still do live in poverty and ignorance, even if their share of the total population has fallen. Would not a consumer sovereignty principle in public services simply leave this group to its fate? Not necessarily. The public power can be used to redistribute resources from the better-off to the poor in the form of cash transfers alone, with all other public services operating as far as feasible on the consumer sovereignty principle. That way (so the standard argument runs) citizens can spend their augmented or depleted fortunes as they think fit in their own interests and cost-related user charges can be levied for the provision of public services.

A cash-transfer system is one way of dealing with the income inequality problem. The other is to make *all* public services redistributive. That means, for instance, free provision of services used heavily by the less well-off, rationing services according to need rather than ability to pay, financing all services out of taxes or making all user charges income-related. This approach certainly makes much heavier inroads into consumer sovereignty and, in orthodox liberal economic argument, is condemned as promoting allocative and productive inefficiency and unnecessarily eroding freedom of choice. By separating payment and consumption, the argument goes, moral hazard appears and waste is encouraged. Offering particular services at no charge is implicitly to judge the least well-off as poor judges of their own interests and to make them less well-off than they would be if given the money equivalent of the service costs. (If they value the services at what those services cost to provide, they would be no worse off with cash instead; if they value the services at less than their cost, they would be better-off with the cash to spend on other things.) By judging needs rather than respecting choices, coercive and intrusive treatment of consumers is encouraged – the bussing of schoolchildren, for instance. By providing services from general taxation rather than from earmarked taxes or user charges, bureaucratic slack is encouraged and incentives set up for producers to exaggerate client 'needs' in order to buttress claims for more budget funds. Such arguments were described in Chapter 4.

A cash-transfer system of redistribution undoubtedly salvages more individual consumer sovereignty than service-specific redistribution. But it has clear drawbacks, too. The most important one is the enforcement issue – the difficulty of making such a cash-transfer system effective, since all the weight of the redistribution effort rests on one administrative mechanism, rather than scattered around public services generally. Partly because of the rule-design problems discussed in Chapter 2, no system of redistributive taxation has yet been devised which does not lend itself to major loopholes and evasion, and the same applies to potential problems of fraud at the cash-receiving end. We need not suppose that the solution to that problem is just around the corner.

Moreover, redistribution by cash transfer alone is a sharp test of the consumer sovereignty principle of taking tastes as given. Suppose that the better-off as a group would like to see extra money go to the poor for medical care but not education. Suppose that the poor as a group would prefer to spend extra money on education but not medical care. Assuming that the poor as a group prefer specific services in kind (free hospital care, say) to nothing at all, then service-specific redistribution will make both groups to some degree better off. But a strictly cash-transfer redistribution system means a clear conflict of group interests, in that one group benefits only to the extent that the other group loses. Collective agreement for the first type of redistribution is thus likely to be easier to obtain than for the second type. (This argument was first advanced by Hochman and Rodgers, 1969.)

Even if the case for specific-service redistribution is accepted, consumer sovereignty can still be built in to the system by voucher-based redistribution in kind rather than administratively allocated services. As mentioned in section I (1), vouchers can be issued which can be exchanged only for specific services, such as education. Now argument (5) is difficult to deploy against voucher schemes; the case against such schemes must rest on argument (1) (possibly (2), (3) or (4) might be invoked too). To the extent that vouchers are not tradeable for other goods (an enforcement problem), a voucher system in principle enables all consumers, rich and poor, to decide what supplier to go to for the service in question. But it may well be difficult to prevent transferability of vouchers except at heavy enforcement cost, as with the school-dinner case discussed in Chapter 3, section II.

III. USER-FRIENDLINESS IN PUBLIC SERVICE PROVISION?

If a pure 'consumer sovereignty' principle cannot (or should not) be applied to all public services, how can producer sovereignty be exercised so as to give top priority to customer convenience? This is an age of convenience foods, armchair shopping, 'user-friendly' intelligent machines. Why not 'convenience administration' or 'user-friendly' public services? Consider four possible ways in which public services might be made 'user-friendly'.

(1) Folksiness

The first, and perhaps most superficial, is to overlay public service provision with a glad-handed aura which conveys at least the appearance of warmth in the relationship of producers and consumers. Public relations devices are used to make consumers feel that they are being treated and valued as 'whole persons' rather than as disembodied cases. The aim is to build up the customer's sense of self-importance rather than diminishing it; and to present the producer as a warm-hearted person rather than a machine – even when the producer *is* a machine. It is now common to programme a hail-fellow-well-met style into machines like computers, telephone answering machines, letter-writing word processors, automatic cash dispensers, so as to give an impression of a 'personalized' warm encounter in what is really nothing of the kind. Indeed it is probably easier to programme such a style into machines than into human agents.

Such artificial folksiness may sometimes irritate or enrage the consumer, especially when it is allied to rigid, highly mechanical treatment in practice (as with those standard recorded telephone messages which give you an apparently 'personal' greeting but do not in fact cover your own case). All the same, an appearance of friendliness and sympathy costs little and may not be unimportant. There is a parallel with the 'human relations' movement of an earlier age, which tried to change the attitude of production workers carrying out repetitive tasks (of a kind increasingly performed by robots) without necessarily changing the reality of their work – for instance, by telling a clerk who filed 4000 police expense claims a day that he was 'helping to fight crime on the streets'. Perhaps something similar may be needed for those who interact to a large degree with enforcement machines and other public service automata, for instance by giving artificial personalities to those machines.

(2) Accessibility

Less superficially, services can be made 'user-friendly' in the sense that that term is used for computer systems. That means service facilities which are inviting, not forbidding, to approach; convenient and easy, not awkward and baffling, to use; which enable users to correct mistakes easily rather than making it difficult and awkward to do so; which require no elaborate training and preparation, no closely-printed 1200-page manual of rules to master before the user can get properly to grips with the system. 'Accessibility', of course, has various dimensions. It may mean physical assessibility: convenient location for consumers (rather than producers), one-stop-shopping, drive-in facilities. It may mean information accessibility, which harks back to the discussion of rule knowability in Chapter 2. That means putting things into plain language rather than jargon, devising simple, step-by-step instructions, algorithms and 'choice of menu' systems, 'designed by geniuses to be used by idiots', and so forth. It may simply mean 'hassle-free service': no endless form-filling, no long waiting times at counter or telephone, no overcrowding, no need for clients to trail from office to office. As with convenience foods, the hard work is done by the producer, not the user.

This, too, can be programmed into machines. It is, of course, one of the big differences between 1950s computer systems and those of the 1980s. It offers a pattern for public administration more generally, and indeed too often opportunities have been lost to introduce more 'convenience administration' on computerization, by simply fitting computers in to a pre-existing procedure rather than fully exploiting their 'user-friendly' potential. The information revolution offers bright prospects for developing convenience administration in this sense. It is more expensive to develop services which are user-friendly in terms of accessibility than it is in terms of folksiness, but the costs tend to be fixed, so that unit costs fall with scale or extent of use rather than rising or staying constant.

(3) Tailor-made Provision

A third possible aspect of user-friendliness is to provide services in the form of a *genuinely* customized or tailor-made product for each user rather than a standard response which lumps all cases together, or treatment of cases in groups rather than separately (as, for instance, in the case of punishment). This goes beyond the apparent personalization of the automatic cash dispenser or recorded telephone message which appears to treat each user individually while in fact treating them identically. It is the 'real thing'.

Now traditionally, this *is* very expensive to produce, and unit costs are proportioned to scale or use, not falling with use, as with accessibility. We have already seen that for services paid for out of taxes, there is a clear conflict between the interest of taxpayers as a group in keeping overall costs down and the interest of each individual user in receiving high-quality 'personalized' service. Every standard text on public administration makes the point that the tendency to routinize and standardize public service provision stems from a need to keep costs down (on the mass-production principle), as well as to ensure equity of treatment and diminish risks of corruption. If you want a customized tax-financed service, the argument runs, taxpayers must be willing to pay more for it, just as if you want a customized automobile, bespoke clothes or shoes, etc. you must be prepared to pay more than for a standard product. The reason why the Model-T Ford was made only in black (as recalled in the epigraph to this chapter) was that high-speed assembly-line production was what made the car affordable to middle-income customers, and at that time the only paint which would dry fast enough to keep up with the production schedule was black. The lack of choice derived from the goal of cheapness, not from an arrogant 'producerist' assumption about what colours people ought to want. (This is argument (4) against consumer choice in section II above.)

However, in manufacturing industry, information technology is changing those traditional assumptions to some extent, in that microprocessors greatly lower the cost of 'customizing'. For instance, a customer can produce his own 'unique' automobile by specifying a particular combination of available units (power unit options, equipment options, colour options) for the assembly-line robots to put together in his case. The cost of this kind of individualization is much less than it would have been (say) 20 years ago. The same factors are at work to cut the relative cost of bespoke clothing and to reduce the transactions cost of individualized contracts, for instance in employment.

In principle, the same technological developments could serve to reduce the production and transaction costs of individualized public services. More complex options could be offered in the realm of tax-and-benefit packages, for instance, without swamping the system of tax and benefit administration. Customized passports, driver licences, marriage certificates might be issued, without costing more than a uniform product. There might be arguments of policy against such 'customizing', but the traditional production cost and transactions cost case against it may become much weaker than it used to be. Here, too, the prospects for increased 'user-friendliness' in public services could be bright.

(4) Minimal Constraint

A fourth possible sense of user-friendliness is to use minimal constraint on citizens in the use of the public power, and so visit on the populace the least possible amount of 'trouble, vexation and oppression', as Adam Smith (1910, p. 309) put it. This phrase perhaps embraces all the senses of user-friendliness discussed here.

Minimal constraint means not using the public power (the authority to permit, prohibit or require) or changes in the physical environment (as with enforcement machines), where less constraining ways of altering behaviour would be equally effective.

Of course, as we have seen throughout this book, there are situations in which using the public power, or constraint through physical action, is unavoidable. At the same time, many public services are provided by little more than information exchange, and trend-spotters have noted an explosion of information-pooling networks in the USA and elsewhere in recent years to foster self-help, share resources, exchange information by groups with interests in common. For instance, in Scotland in the lambing season, some local radio stations work as informational clearing-houses, so that motherless lambs can be matched with ewes in milk whose lambs have died. No one is being forced to do anything. Any 'authority' involved in this public service is *auctoritas suadendi* and no more.

Similarly, many public services rely mainly on financial incentives and disincentives to shape citizens' action, such as fines, grants, loads on insurance premium payments. Again, constraint on the citizen is fairly low. The individual can decide whether it is worth paying a fine (say, for pollution or illegal parking) rather than observing a rule, or whether to take up a 'cash with strings' offer or not. Part of the traditional case for fines as preferable to punishments in kind is that low constraint conveys maximal freedom of choice and promotes allocative efficiency (see Chapter 3). The case for benefits in money rather than in kind is a mirror-image of the same argument.

A minimal constraint principle would dictate that lower constraint instruments of public policy (information networking and financial incentives) be preferred to higher constraint instruments (authority and physical action) where all else is equal.

In many cases, this principle is also a way of keeping production costs down. For instance, information networking tends to be fairly cheap and perhaps is becoming increasingly so, with the telecommunications revolution. It does not depend much on resources which are used up as they are used. That, however, rarely applies to enforcement machines and physical treatment, which tends to be much more expensive in people, money and materials. Fines are a far cheaper form of punishment than incarceration.

But, as with customizing service, the aim of keeping producer costs down in some cases conflicts with the minimal constraint principle. In particular, trying to influence social behaviour by offering financial incentives, though low in constraint, is far more expensive to the producer than using the public power to compel behaviour in such a way that the costs of compliance are borne by citizens at large. In this case, it is the higher constraint instrument, not the lower constraint one, which does not use up the resources on which it is based as it uses them. Moreover, unlike (perhaps) customizing service, the information revolution is not likely to change those relativities much. In this case, some aspects of 'user-friendliness' involve potentially higher production costs than 'user-unfriendliness' (see Hood, 1983, pp. 144–5).

IV. CONCLUSION

The 'fiduciary trustee' style of public service provision seems to command less automatic support than it once did, even in countries where there has traditionally been an emphasis on this approach. But we cannot always opt for full-blooded consumer sovereignty as an alternative, for reasons which have been stressed throughout this book and briefly rehearsed in section I above. All the same, trusteeship can be exercised in a variety of styles, in terms of the relationship between the trustees and the beneficiaries. In particular, a style of public service provision which stops far short of complete consumer sovereignty might still be to some extent user-friendly. In many cases that need not involve vastly more expensive public services than would apply to a user-unfriendly style of provision. In many cases, too, the prospects for extension of this approach look encouraging. If we cannot make public services consumer-driven, we may at least be able to make them more user-friendly.

QUESTIONS FOR REVIEW

1. Commuters at a bus station repeatedly complain of overcrowding, lack of facilities and poor maintenance. PR spokesmen for the bus company respond that there is no room for expansion of public facilities, since vacant space on the site is earmarked for a new car park and health club for company staff; and that an upgrading of

existing facilities would anyway only attract vagrants and drug addicts. Without knowing any more details about the situation, what institutional changes might you suggest to make the bus company more responsive to its consumers?

2. How far do you think it is feasible to carry the principle of consumer sovereignty in the field of:

   (a) Fire services?
   (b) Radio and TV broadcasting? .
   (c) Primary education?
   (d) Crime prevention?

3. You have to apply in person to collect money which is legally due to you from a public bureaucracy. The office is right on the outskirts of town, closes for a long lunch hour, and there is no system for making appointments in advance, so you have to give up a good deal of time to make the trip. When you arrive, there is nowhere to park and you are not allowed to use the lift, which is for staff only. After climbing four flights of stairs, the signposting to the repayment section gives out, and you get lost. Eventually, two flights further up, you find the right room, and take your place in a slow-moving queue of about 75 people. The room has no seats and ventilation is poor. When you finally reach the head of the queue, the clerk taps your details into a computer, and makes you fill in several complicated forms, the purpose of which is not explained. Instead of giving you the money, however, he then directs you to another long, slowly-moving queue. When, over an hour later, you finally reach the repayment window, you are told that you have failed to give the required 14 days notice of repayment (a fact which is not advertised, and which the first clerk did not tell you), and that, after standing in line to fill in the necessary forms in a different office to lodge your claim for repayment, you must go through the entire process again in a fortnight. Just as you breathlessly reach the notice of repayment office, you are told that the office is closing for the day (it is 3 p.m.).

In what ways could this hypothetical repayment process be made more 'user-friendly'?

GUIDE TO FURTHER READING

Of books championing the 'consumer' approach to public service provision in opposition to the traditional producer-oriented approach, Ostrom (1974) is probably still the most trenchant and radical. Macrae (1984) is an entertaining social sci-fi story, purporting to show how changes in information technology can tip the balance of public service provision towards increased consumer orientation. It is based to some degree on Naisbitt (1982), whose ideas about information networking, high touch and the individuating potential of modern information technology have been heavily drawn upon here. The theme of minimizing 'constraint' on citizens in the use of administrative resources is treated at more length than is possible here by Hood (1983) and also by Dunsire (in Klinkers, 1985, pp. 64–72), though many of the underlying principles derive from Adam Smith and Bentham (1931, pp. 326, 329, 332, 338, 353). Rourke (1976, p. 149 and passim) makes some perceptive observations on the paradoxes involved in seeking to make public bureaucracies more 'responsive' to clients.

References

Albrow, N. (1970) *Bureaucracy* (London, Pall Mall Press).

Allott, A. (1980) *The Limits of Law* (London, Butterworths).

Ashby, W. R. (1956) *An Introduction to Cybernetics* (London, Chapman and Hall).

Bardach, E. and Kagan, R. A. (1982) *Going By The Book: The Problem of Regulatory Unreasonableness* (Philadelphia, Temple University Press).

Beattie, J. M. (1967) *The English Court in the Reign of George I* (Cambridge, Cambridge University Press).

Becker, G. S. (1968) 'Crime and Punishment: An Economic Approach', *Journal of Political Economy* **76**, 169–217.

Becker, G. S. and Stigler, G. J. (1974) 'Law Enforcement, Malfeasance and Compensation of Enforcers', *Journal of Legal Studies* **3**, 1–17.

Beer, S. (1966) *Decision and Control* (London, Wiley).

Beer, S. (1975) *Platform for Change* (London, Wiley).

Bennett, J. M. (1983) 'Large Computer Project Problems and their Causes', *Australian Computer Bulletin* **7**, 18–28.

Bentham, J. (1931) *The Theory of Legislation*, ed. C. K. Ogden, tr. R. Hildreth from the French of E. Dumont (London, Routledge and Kegan Paul).

Bernstein, M. (1955) *Regulating Business by Independent Commission* (Princeton, Princeton University Press).

Boswell, J. (1909) *The Journal of a Tour to the Hebrides with Samuel Johnson LL.D.* (London, J. M. Dent and Sons).

Brennan, G. and Pincus, J. (1983) *The Growth of Government: Do The Figures Tell Us What We Want To Know?*', in Taylor (1980), pp. 33–49.

Breton, A. (1974) *The Economic Theory of Representative Government* (London, Macmillan).

Breyer, S. (1982) *Regulation and its Reform* (Cambridge, Mass., Harvard University Press).

Clark, L. (1975) *The Grand Jury: The Use and Abuse of Political Power* (New York, Quadrangle/The *New York Times* Book Co.).

Cmnd. 6734 (1976) *119th Report of the Board of Inland Revenue* (London, HMSO).

Cmnd. 8610 (1982) *The Future of Telecommunications in Britain* (London, HMSO).

Coase, R. H. (1960) 'The Problem of Social Cost', *Journal of Law and Economics* **3**, 1–44.

Crain, W. M. and Ekelund, R. B. (1976) 'Chadwick and Demsetz on Competition and Regulation', *Journal of Law and Economics* **19**, 149–62.

Cranston, R. (1979) *Regulating Business: Law and Consumer Agencies* (London, Macmillan).

Crozier, M. (1964) *The Bureaucratic Phenomenon* (Chicago, Chicago University Press).

Demsetz, H. (1968) 'Why Regulate Utilities?', *Journal of Law and Economics* **11**, 55–65.

Deutsch, K. W. (1963) *The Nerves of Government* (New York, Free Press).

Downs, A. (1967) *Inside Bureaucracy* (New York, Wiley).

Dunsire, A. (1973) *Administration, The Word and the Science* (London, Martin Robertson).

Dunsire, A. (1978a) *The Execution Process, Vol. 1: Implementation in a Bureaucracy* (Oxford, Martin Robertson).

Dunsire, A. (1978b) *The Execution Process. Vol. 2: Control in a Bureaucracy* (Oxford, Martin Robertson).

Dunsire, A. (1980) 'Implementation Theory', Paper 12, The Open University, Social Sciences: A Third Level Course, *Policies, People and Administration*, Block 3, *Implementation, Evaluation and Change*.

Dunsire, A. (1985) 'Why Administer? The Moral Dimension of Administrative Reform', in Klinkers (1985), pp. 64–72.

Elster, J. (1983) 'The Crisis in Economic Theory', *London Review of Books*, 20 October/2 November, 5–7.

Fenn, P. and Veljanovski, C. J. (1983) 'A Positive Economic Theory of Regulatory Enforcement', Paper presented to conference on 'Regulation in Britain', Oxford, 12 September 1983.

Freedman, J. O. (1978) *Crisis and Legitimacy* (Cambridge, Cambridge University Press).

Friedman, D (1979) 'Private Creation and Enforcement of Law: A Historical Case', *Journal of Legal Studies* **8**, 399–415.

Friedman, M. and Friedman, R. (1980) *Free To Choose* (London, Secker and Warburg).

Fuller, L. (1967) *Legal Fictions* (Stanford, Calif., Stanford University Press).

Gatti, J. F. (1981) *The Limits of Government Regulation* (New York, Academic Press).

Gaus, J. (1947) *Reflections on Public Administration* (Alabama, Alabama University Press).

Gerth, H. H. and Mills, C. W. (1948) *From Max Weber: Essays in Sociology* (London, Routledge and Kegan Paul).

Gibson, J. S. (1985) *The Thistle and the Crown: A History of the Scottish Office* (Edinburgh, HMSO).

Gottlieb, G. (1968) *The Logic of Choice: An Investigation of the Concepts of Rule and Rationality* (London, Allen and Unwin).

Griffith, J. A. G. and Street, H. (1952) *Principles of Administrative Law* (London, Pitman (many later editions)).

Gustaffson, B. (1979) *Post-Industrial Society* (London, Croom Helm).

Hanf, K. and Scharpf, F. W. (1978) *Interorganizational Policy-Making* (London, Sage).

Hardin, G. (1968) 'The Tragedy of the Commons', *Science 162* (December 1968), 1243–8.

Hart, H. L. A. (1961) *The Concept of Law* (Oxford, Clarendon Press).

Hawkins, K. E. and Thomas, J. M. (1984) 'The Enforcement Process in Regulatory Bureaucracies', in Hawkins and Thomas (1984), 3–22.

Hawkins, K. E. and Thomas, J. (1984) *Enforcing Regulation* (Boston, Kluwer-Nijhoff).

Heald, D. A. (1983) *Public Expenditure* (Oxford, Martin Robertson).

Hirschman, A. O. (1970) *Exit Voice and Loyalty* (Cambridge, Mass., Harvard University Press).

Hjern, B. and Porter, D. O. (1981) 'Implementation Structures: A New Unit of Administrative Analysis', *Organization Studies* 2, 211–27.

Hochman, H. H. and Rodgers, J. R. (1969) 'Pareto-Optimal Redistribution', *American Economic Review* 59, 542–57.

Hood, C. C. (1976) *The Limits of Administration* (London, Wiley).

Hood, C. C. and Wright, M. (1981) *Big Government in Hard Times* (Oxford, Martin Robertson).

Hood, C. C. (1983) *The Tools of Government* (London, Macmillan).

Hood, C. C. (1985) 'British Tax Structure Change as Administrative Adaptation', *Policy Sciences* 18, 3–31.

Illich, I. (1972) *Deschooling Society* (London, Calder and Boyars).

Jackson, P. M. (1982) *The Political Economy of Bureaucracy* (Oxford, Phillip Allan).

Jarvis, R. C. (1973) 'Ship Registry 1707–86', in R. Craig (ed.), *Maritime History*, Vol. 2 (Newton Abbott, David and Charles), pp. 151–67.

Jewkes, J., Sawers, D. and Stillerman, R. (1969) *The Sources of Invention*, 2nd edn (London, Macmillan).

Jowell, J. L. (1975) *Law and Bureaucracy: Administrative Discretion and the Limits of Legal Action* (New York, Dunellan and Kennikat Press).

Kagan, R. A. (1978) *Regulatory Justice: Implementing a Wage–Price Freeze* (New York, Russell Sage Foundation).

Kagan, R. A. and Scholz, J. T. (1984) 'The Criminology of the Corporation and Regulatory Enforcement Strategies', in Hawkins and Thomas (1984), pp. 67–95.

Katzenbach, E. (1958) 'The Horse Cavalry in the Twentieth Century: A Study in Policy Response', *Public Policy*, 120–49.

Kaufmann, F.-X., Ostrom, V. and Majone, G. (1986) *Guidance, Control and Performance Evaluation in the Public Sector* (Berlin, de Gruyter).

Kay, J. A. and King, M. (1980) *The British Tax System*, 2nd edn (Oxford, Oxford University Press).

Kelman, S. 'Enforcement of Occupational Safety and Health Regulations: A Comparison of Swedish and American Practices', in Hawkins and Thomas (1984), pp. 97–119.

Klinkers, L. (ed.) (1985) *Life in Public Administration* (Amsterdam, Kobra).

Kochen, M. and Deutsch, K. W. (1980) *Decentralization* (Cambridge, Mass., Oelgeschlager, Gunn and Hain).

Landes, W. M. and Posner, R. A. (1975) 'The Private Enforcement of Law', *Journal of Legal Studies* **4**, 1–46.

Landis, J. (1938) *The Administrative Process* (New Haven, Yale University Press).

Laver, M. (1983) *Invitation to Politics* (Oxford, Martin Robertson).

Leibenstein, H. (1976) *Beyond Economic Man: A New Foundation for Microeconomics* (Cambridge, Mass., Harvard University Press).

Levene, T. (1983) 'Who Wants to Be a Part-Time Millionaire?', *Sunday Times*, 25 September 1983, p. 63.

Low, T. J. (1969) *The End of Liberalism* (New York, Norton).

MacDonagh, O. (1961) *A Pattern of Government Growth 1800–60* (London, MacGibbon and Kee).

Macrae, N. (1984) *The 2024 Report: A Concise History of the Future 1974–2024* (London, Sidgwick and Jackson).

Majone, G. (1980) 'Process and Outcome in Regulatory Decision-Making', in Weiss and Barton (1980), pp. 235–58.

March, J. G. and Simon, H. A. (1958) *Organizations* (New York, Wiley).

Marshall, G. (1984) *Constitutional Conventions: The Rules and Forms of Political Accountability* (Oxford, Clarendon Press).

Martin, S. (1983) *Managing Without Managers: Alternative Work Arrangements in Public Organization* (Beverley Hills, Sage).

Mashaw, J. L. (1983) *Bureaucratic Justice: Managing Social Security Disability Claims* (New Haven, Yale University Press).

Minasian, J. R. (1969) 'The Political Economy of Broadcasting in the 1920s', *Journal of Law and Economics* **12**, 391–43.

Mueller, D. C. (1979) *Public Choice* (Cambridge, Cambridge University Press).

Naisbitt, J. (1982) *Megatrends: Ten New Directions Transforming Our Lives* (New York, Warner Books).

Nelson, R. and Winter, S. (1982) *An Evolutionary Theory of Economic Change* (Cambridge, Mass., Harvard University Press).

Niskanen, W. A. (1971) *Bureaucracy and Representative Government* (Chicago, Aldine Atherton).

Niskanen, W. A. (1975) 'Bureaucrats and Politicians', *Journal of Law and Economics* **18**, 617–43.

Niskanen, W. A. (1980) 'Competition among Government Bureaus', in Weiss and Barton (1980), pp. 167–74.

Olson, M. (1971) *The Logic of Collective Action: Public Goods and the Theory of Groups*, rev. edn (New York, Schocken Books).

Ostrom, E. (1981) 'Modeling Incentive Systems in Public Bureaus', Paper presented to conference on 'Guidance, Control and Performance Evaluation in the Public Sector', Centre for Interdisciplinary Research, University of Bielefeld, Federal Republic of Germany, 14–19 October 1981.

Ostrom, E. (1984) 'An Agenda for the Study of Institutions', Presidential address delivered at the Public Choice Society Meetings, Hilton Hotel, Phoenix, Arizona, 30 March 1984.

Ostrom, E., Parks, R. B. and Whitaker, G. P. (1977) *Policing Metropolitan America* (Washington, DC, US Government Printing Office).

Ostrom, E., Parks, R. B. and Whitaker, G. P. (1978) *Patterns of Metropolitan Policing* (Cambridge, Mass., Ballinger).

Ostrom, V. (1974) *The Intellectual Crisis in American Public Administration* rev. edn (Alabama, University of Alabama Press).

Ostrom, V. (1975) 'Comment' (on R. E. Wagner and W. E. Weber, 'Competition, Monopoly and the Organization of Government in Metropolitan Areas'), *Journal of Law and Economics* **18**, 691–4.

Ostrom, V. (1982) 'Adam Smith and Public Goods', Paper to Adam Smith Colloquium, Centre for Interdisciplinary Research, University of Bielefeld, Federal Republic of Germany, 23–26 February 1982.

Ostrom, V. (1984), 'Constitutional Considerations with Particular Reference to Federal Systems', in Kaufmann, Ostrom and Majone (1986) pp. 111–25.

Ostrom, V. and Ostrom, E. (1978) 'Public Goods and Public Choices' in Savas (1978), pp. 7–49.

Ostrom, V., Tiebout, C. M. and Warren, R. (1961) 'The Organization of Government in Metropolitan Areas: A Theoretical Inquiry', *American Political Science Review* **55**, 831–42.

Parks, R. B. and Ostrom, E. (1982) 'A "Classical" Theory of the Public Bureau', Centre for Interdisciplinary Research, University of Bielefeld, Federal Republic of Germany, Discussion Paper No. 21 in 'Guidance Control and Performance Evaluation in the Public Sector' series.

Peacock, A. T. (1979) 'Public Expenditure Growth in Post-Industrial Society', in Gustaffson (1979), pp. 80–95.

Perrow, C. (1979) *Complex Organizations: A Critical Essay*, 2nd edn (Glenview, Ill., Scott, Foresman).

Pollitt, C (1984) 'Professionals and Public Policy', *Public Administration Bulletin*, No. 44 (April 1984), 29–46.

Posner, R. A. (1977) *Economic Analysis of Law*, 2nd edn (Boston, Little, Brown).

Pressman, J. and Wildavsky, A. (1973) *Implementation* (Berkeley, University of California Press).

Reiss, A. J. (1984) 'Selecting Strategies of Social Control over Organizational Life', in Hawkins and Thomas (1984), pp. 23–35.

Roalman, A. R. (1968) 'How Sweden Won the Big Traffic Battle', *Public Relations Journal* (February 1968).

Rose, R. (1985) 'The Growth of Government Organizations: Do We Count The Number or Weigh the Programmes?' *Studies in Public Policy* No. 148 (Glasgow, University of Strathclyde).

Rosenberg, N. (1960) 'Some Institutional Aspects of the Wealth of Nations', *Journal of Political Economy* **68**, 557–70.

Rourke, F. E. (1976) *Bureaucracy, Politics and Public Policy*, 2nd edn (Boston, Little, Brown).

Rourke, F. E. (1980) 'Bureaucratic Autonomy and the Public Interest', in Weiss and Barton (1980), pp. 103–12.

Samuels, W. J. and Schmid, A. A. (1981) *Law and Economics: An Institutional Perspective* (Boston/The Hague/London, Martinus Nijhoff).

Savas, E. S. (1977) *The Organization and Efficiency of Solid Waste Collection* (Lexington, Mass., Lexington Books).

Savas, E. S. (1978) *Alternatives for Delivering Public Services: Towards Improved Performance* (Boulder, Colorado, Westview Press).

Schaffer, B. (1973) *The Administrative Factor* (London, Frank Cass).

Schmid, A. A. (1981) 'Predicting the Performance of Alternative Institutions', in Samuels and Schmid (1981), pp. 76–94.

Schumpeter, J. (1954) *Capitalism, Socialism and Democracy*, 4th edn (London, Allen and Unwin).

Scigliano, R. (1971) *The Supreme Court and the Presidency* (New York, Free Press).

Sennett, R. (1977) *The Fall of Public Man* (Cambridge, Cambridge University Press).

Sharpe, L. J. (1986) 'Intergovernmental Policy-Making: The Limits of Sub-National Autonomy', in Kaufmann, Ostrom and Majone (1986), pp. 159–81.

Sheckley, R. (1974) *The Same to You Doubled* (London, Pan Books).

Silver, N. (1967) 'Ambidextrous Sweden', *New Statesman* 15 September 1967.

Simon, H. A., Smithburg, D. W. and Thompson, V. A. (1950) *Public Administration*, (New York, Alfred Knopf).

Smith, A. (1910) *The Wealth of Nations* (London, J. M. Dent).

Smith, A. (1937) *The Wealth of Nations* (New York, Modern Library Edition, Random House).

Smith, A. (1978) *Lectures on Jurisprudence* ed. R. L. Meed, D. D. Raphael, and P. G. Stein (Oxford, Clarendon Press).

Sowell, T. (1981) 'Poverty, the Distribution of Income and Social Policy: Some Thoughts', in Gatti (1981), pp. 35–56.

Statens Hogertrafikkommission (The National Swedish Commission for Right-Hand Traffic) (1967), Follow-up Team, 'Road-Users Adaptation to Right-Hand Traffic', unpublished report (Stockholm, 20 November 1967).

Steel, T. (1975) *The Life and Death of St Kilda* (Glasgow, Fontana).

Steinbruner, J. D. (1974) *The Cybernetic Theory of Decision: New Dimensions of Political Analysis* (Princeton, Princeton University Press).

Stigler, G. J. (1958) 'The Economics of Scale', *Journal of Law and Economics* 1, pp. 54–71.

Stigler, G. J. (1964) 'Public Regulation of the Securities Market', *Journal of Business* 37, 117–42.

Stigler, G. J (1970) 'The Optimum Enforcement of Laws', *Journal of Political Economy* 78, 526–36.

Stone, D. (1975) *Where the Law Ends: The Social Control of Corporate Behaviour* (New York, Harper and Row).

Taylor, C. L. (1983) *Why Governments Grow: Measuring Public Sector Size* (Beverly Hills, Sage).

Thompson, V. A. (1975) *Without Sympathy or Enthusiasm* (Alabama, University of Alabama Press).

Toqueville, A. de (1949) *L'Ancien Regime* (Oxford, Clarendon Press).

Tullock, G. (1965) *The Politics of Bureaucracy* (Washington, DC, Public Affairs Press).

Turner, B. (1976) 'How to Manage Disaster', *Management Today* (March), 56–7, 105.

Turner, B. (1978) *Man-made Disasters* (London, Wykeman).

Twining, W. and Miers, D. (1976) *How To Do Things With Rules: A Primer of Interpretation* (London, Weidenfeld and Nicolson).

Veblen, T. (1966) *Imperial Germany and the Industrial Revolution* (Michigan University Press).

Veljanovski, C. G. (1984) 'The Economics of Regulatory Enforcement', in Hawkins and Thomas (1984), pp. 171–88.

von Mises, L. (1944) *Bureaucracy* (New Haven, Yale University Press).

Wade, E. C. S. (1982) *Administrative Law*, 5th edn (Oxford, Clarendon Press).

Wagner, R. E. (1973) *The Public Economy* (Chicago, Markham).

Weiss, C. H. and Barton, A. H. (eds) (1980) *Making Bureaucracies Work* (Beverly Hills, Sage).

Wildavsky, A. (1979) *Speaking Truth to Power* (New York, Macmillan).

Williams, R. (1980) *The Nuclear Power Decisions* (London, Croom Helm).

Williamson, O. E. (1975) *Markets and Hierarchies* (London, Collier Macmillan).

Wilson, W. (1887) 'The Study of Administration', *Political Science Quarterly* **2**, 197–222.

Index

203